DK experience

VOLCANO

written by
ANNE ROONEY

HOW IT HAPPENED...

POMPEII

BURIED UNDER BURNING VOLCANIC ASH

The fiery winds bursting from Vesuvius have inspired many artists. Pierre Jacques Volaire painted this scene soon after the volcano erupted again in 1785.

Italy

Vesuvius

Naples
Herculaneum • Pompeii

*MEDITERRANEAN
SEA*

Animals died where they fell. This dog was covered in ash, which hardened around the animal. When its body rotted away, a hollow was left. Centuries later, liquid plaster was poured in to make a cast.

No-one living in the Ancient Roman cities of Pompeii and Herculaneum in southern Italy had any idea that the mountain towering above them was an active volcano. When it blew itself apart in August AD 79, it brought rapid death to many of the 25,000 people living in its shadow.

"Ashes were already falling, hotter and thicker as the ships drew near, followed by bits of pumice."

Roman historian Pliny the Younger, 17 years old when he witnessed the eruption from a town across the bay

burned by falling ash so thick that it blocked out the sun. Others were crushed by falling buildings as they sheltered from the volcanic rocks (called pumice) and scalding ash raining down on them. Scorching winds that swept down the slopes of Vesuvius may have ripped through Pompeii to the beach, vaporizing victims instantly.

Death in the streets

As the volcano began to pour smoke, ash, and red-hot rock into the air, thousands of people fled their homes in Pompeii. Many died in the streets or on the beach as they frantically tried to escape by sea across the Bay of Naples. They were overcome by hot, poisonous gases or

Vanishing act

Nearby, searing blasts of hot ash and gases tore through the wealthy town of Herculaneum. These blistering winds buried the ruined town under a flood of ash, pumice, and volcanic mud up to 20 m (65 ft) deep. Most of Herculaneum remains buried to this day.

"Of the unfortunates found here, nothing remains of their flesh but the imprints in the ground..."

Archaeologist Francesco La Vega, noting what he discovered at one of Pompeii's villas in December 1772

POMPEII TIMELINE

AD 62 A large earthquake topples buildings in Pompeii. Many of them had only just been restored when the great volcanic eruption struck 17 years later.

24 August AD 79 Loud explosions inside Vesuvius.
1.00 pm A column of gas 15 km (9 miles) high and laced with lightning soars into the sky.
1.00–8.00 pm Ash and volcanic rocks rain down.

25 August Vesuvius continues to erupt.
1.00 am The gas column collapses and superheated winds roar down the slopes of Vesuvius towards Herculaneum.
7.30 am More fiery winds consume Pompeii's remains.

Deadly spectacle

Curious observers stayed to watch, some even risking their lives by going closer. No survivors left first-hand accounts of how Pompeii and Herculaneum were destroyed. But Pliny the Younger wrote detailed observations of the eruption from across the Bay of Naples. His account gives a powerful insight into the terrible events, and has been useful to modern historians and scientists. His uncle, Pliny the Elder, died on the beach watching the eruption.

Preserved under ash

The city of Pompeii was buried by a layer of stone and ash 4.5–7.5 m (15–25 ft) thick. Soon, new grass and trees grew in the fertile soil and covered the site. It lay hidden for 1,500 years until builders uncovered carved slabs of marble, but it remained unexplored until 1748. Early digging was carried out by slaves chained in pairs.

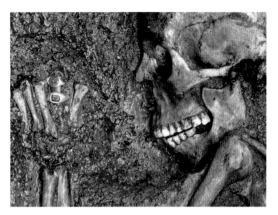

A skeleton uncovered at Herculaneum still wears two rings. Preserved artefacts and buildings found at the two cities have given us a fascinating picture of Ancient Roman life.

Many victims were discovered huddled together. Scientists believe that they died suddenly, engulfed by a surge of burning gas.

"How *very* horrible: the certainty that such a scene may be acted all over again tomorrow."

Hester Thrale, an English woman who visited the ruins after another great eruption shook the area in 1785

Many died when they broke into pockets of poisonous gas trapped under the surface. Excavators found street after street of buildings preserved under the ash. Hollow spaces in the hardened ash revealed the shapes of bodies, long gone, of the people who died in the eruption. Casts have been made by pouring plaster or resin into these spaces left by the victims' bodies. As soon as news of the excavations spread, Pompeii began to attract visitors from around the world.

Eruptions continue

Today, two-thirds of the city inside Pompeii's walls are still buried. Most of Herculaneum lies under mud hardened to rock, and some of it is far beneath the modern town of Resina, whose residents live within lava-flow distance of Vesuvius. Worryingly, the volcano continues to erupt – it has done so more than 50 times since AD 79.

In March 1944, ash clouds billowed out of Vesuvius again, in the worst eruption for 70 years. Lava flows destroyed the nearby towns of Massa and San Sebastiano.

Devastating facts

The eruption of Vesuvius tore the mountain apart and devastated the surrounding towns and villages. Many people fled their homes, but they had to face a horrendous onslaught from the volcano.

Big bang	The eruption was the type known as Plinian. It released 100,000 times more energy than the atomic bomb that destroyed the Japanese city of Hiroshima at the end of World War II.
Deadly cloud	A column of gas, ash, and rock spurted 15 km (9 miles) straight up into the sky, spreading out in a shape like a giant umbrella.
Tonnes of rock	At the height of the eruption, Vesuvius shot 150,000 tonnes of rock into the air every second – a total of 2.6 km³ (0.6 cu miles).
Searing wind	Six blasts of scalding wind carrying ash and poisonous gases rushed down the mountainside at up to 100 km/h (62 mph).
Scorched	The wind reached temperatures of up to 800°C (1,470°F) – hot enough to turn wood to carbon in an instant.
Hail of stones	For 18 hours, Pompeii was bombarded by pumice stones that piled up into a layer 2.5 m (8 ft) deep.
Buried	By the end of the eruption, Pompeii lay buried under 4.5–7.5 m (15–25 ft) of debris. To the west of the mountain, Herculaneum was left 20 m (65 ft) underground.
Destroyed	Half of Vesuvius disappeared when its summit collapsed, leaving a hole 3 km (1.8 miles) wide.
Victims	Most victims of the explosion died from terrible burns, were suffocated, or were crushed alive.

1592 Coins and marble fragments are found at Pompeii.
1689 A carved marble slab discovered underground alerts people to the existence of the ruins of Pompeii.
1709 A workman digs up marble from Herculaneum.

1748 Large-scale excavations begin at Pompeii.
1765 Excavators start to map the buildings they uncover.
1860 Work shifts from treasure-hunting to detailed scientific investigation.

EARTH IS FORMED

The story of the Earth's volcanoes begins more than 4,000 million years ago when the planet was first forming. Nearly 10,000 million years after the Universe exploded into existence, the Solar System emerged from a whirling cloud of gas and dust. The centre of the cloud collapsed and ignited, forming a new star – our Sun. Over millions of years, the Earth and the other rocky planets grew from the dense, solid matter closest to the Sun. Beneath its surface, the interior of the young Earth was in turmoil – and it still is. Every day, in spectacular and often devastating eruptions, volcanoes release gas and molten rock that may have been trapped inside the planet for millions of years.

As a massive collection of rocks and ice whirled around the Sun, pieces clumped together to form planetesimals. Over a period of 10–100 million years they grew into planets by crashing together and sweeping up loose pieces of debris.

At the edge of the new Solar System, the first planets emerged. Known as the gas giants, Jupiter, Saturn, Uranus, and Neptune were formed from the less dense material that was thrown far away from the Sun. These planets are mostly liquid gas, with a rocky centre.

Millions of lumps of rock and metal called asteroids escaped as the planets developed. Most circle the Sun between Jupiter and Mars, forming the asteroid belt, but some travel closer to Earth. Asteroids can measure up to 1,000 km (620 miles) across.

molten When rock is heated to melting point.

Solar System The Sun and the nine planets that revolve around it, along with their moons, asteroids, and comets.

asteroids Chunks of rock and iron that are orbiting the Sun. They are sometimes known as minor planets.

gravity The force exerted by a heavy body, such as a planet, which pulls other objects towards its centre.

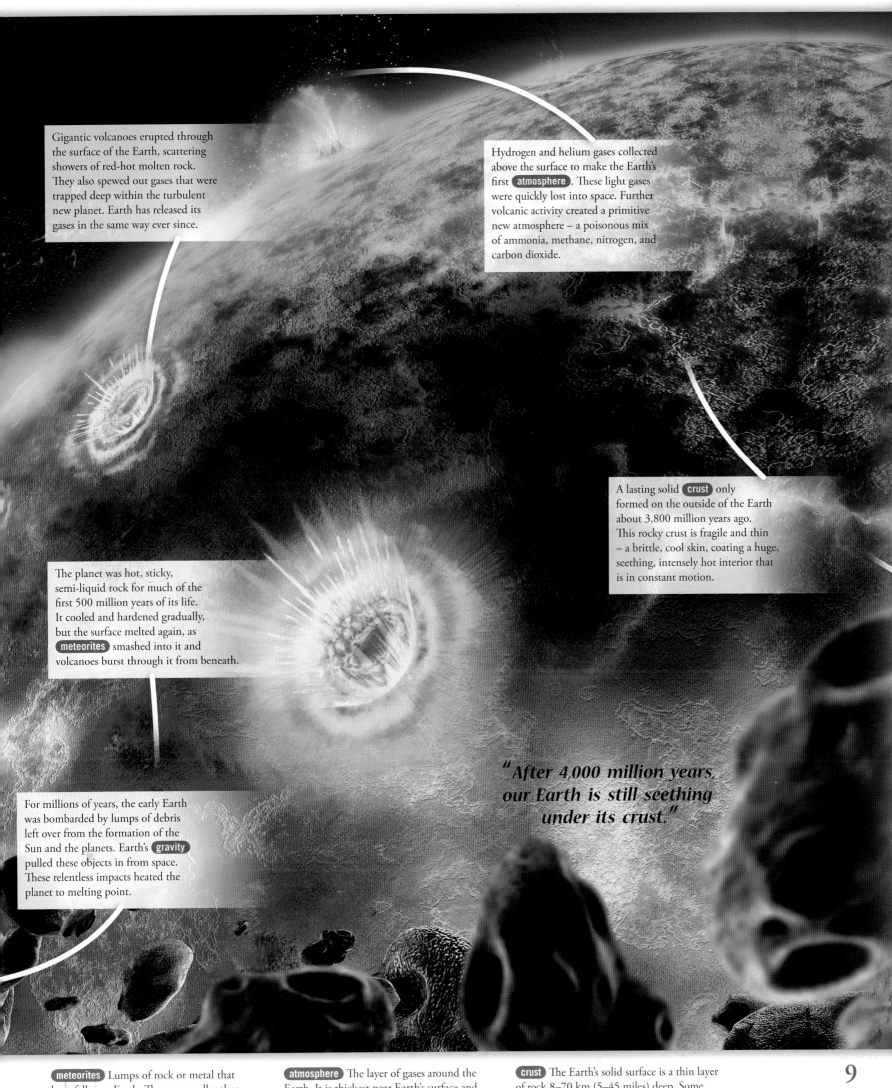

Gigantic volcanoes erupted through the surface of the Earth, scattering showers of red-hot molten rock. They also spewed out gases that were trapped deep within the turbulent new planet. Earth has released its gases in the same way ever since.

Hydrogen and helium gases collected above the surface to make the Earth's first **atmosphere**. These light gases were quickly lost into space. Further volcanic activity created a primitive new atmosphere – a poisonous mix of ammonia, methane, nitrogen, and carbon dioxide.

A lasting solid **crust** only formed on the outside of the Earth about 3,800 million years ago. This rocky crust is fragile and thin – a brittle, cool skin, coating a huge, seething, intensely hot interior that is in constant motion.

The planet was hot, sticky, semi-liquid rock for much of the first 500 million years of its life. It cooled and hardened gradually, but the surface melted again, as **meteorites** smashed into it and volcanoes burst through it from beneath.

"After 4,000 million years, our Earth is still seething under its crust."

For millions of years, the early Earth was bombarded by lumps of debris left over from the formation of the Sun and the planets. Earth's **gravity** pulled these objects in from space. These relentless impacts heated the planet to melting point.

meteorites Lumps of rock or metal that have fallen to Earth. They are smaller than asteroids – some are as tiny as a grain of sand.

atmosphere The layer of gases around the Earth. It is thickest near Earth's surface and extends to about 700 km (435 miles) high.

crust The Earth's solid surface is a thin layer of rock 8–70 km (5–45 miles) deep. Some crust is covered by sea water.

9

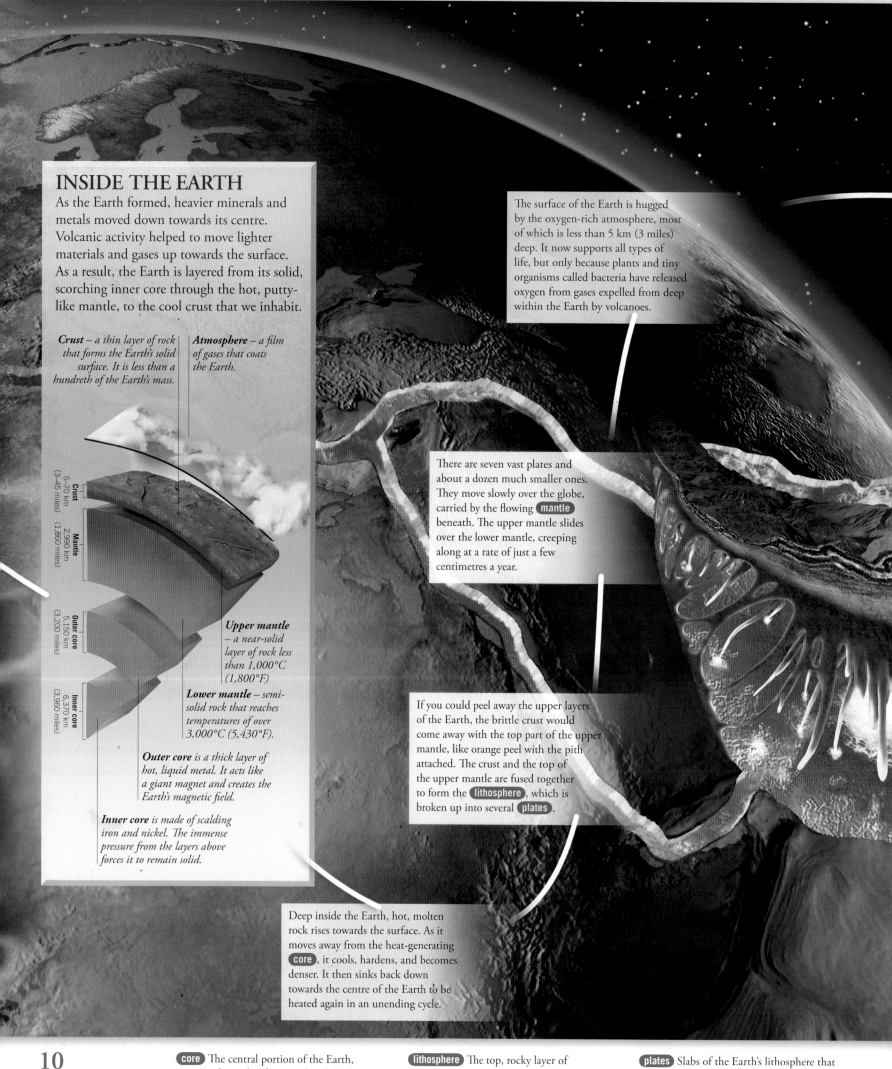

INSIDE THE EARTH

As the Earth formed, heavier minerals and metals moved down towards its centre. Volcanic activity helped to move lighter materials and gases up towards the surface. As a result, the Earth is layered from its solid, scorching inner core through the hot, putty-like mantle, to the cool crust that we inhabit.

Crust – a thin layer of rock that forms the Earth's solid surface. It is less than a hundreth of the Earth's mass.

Atmosphere – a film of gases that coats the Earth.

Upper mantle – a near-solid layer of rock less than 1,000°C (1,800°F)

Lower mantle – semi-solid rock that reaches temperatures of over 3,000°C (5,430°F).

Outer core is a thick layer of hot, liquid metal. It acts like a giant magnet and creates the Earth's magnetic field.

Inner core is made of scalding iron and nickel. The immense pressure from the layers above forces it to remain solid.

Crust 5–70 km (3–45 miles)

Mantle 2,990 km (1,860 miles)

Outer core 5,150 km (3,200 miles)

Inner core 6,370 km (3,960 miles)

The surface of the Earth is hugged by the oxygen-rich atmosphere, most of which is less than 5 km (3 miles) deep. It now supports all types of life, but only because plants and tiny organisms called bacteria have released oxygen from gases expelled from deep within the Earth by volcanoes.

There are seven vast plates and about a dozen much smaller ones. They move slowly over the globe, carried by the flowing mantle beneath. The upper mantle slides over the lower mantle, creeping along at a rate of just a few centimetres a year.

If you could peel away the upper layers of the Earth, the brittle crust would come away with the top part of the upper mantle, like orange peel with the pith attached. The crust and the top of the upper mantle are fused together to form the lithosphere, which is broken up into several plates.

Deep inside the Earth, hot, molten rock rises towards the surface. As it moves away from the heat-generating core, it cools, hardens, and becomes denser. It then sinks back down towards the centre of the Earth to be heated again in an unending cycle.

10

core The central portion of the Earth, composed mainly of iron and nickel. The outer core is liquid, the inner core is solid.

lithosphere The top, rocky layer of the Earth. It includes the top of the upper mantle and the solid crust.

plates Slabs of the Earth's lithosphere that fit together to cover the planet. Most large plates carry both land and ocean.

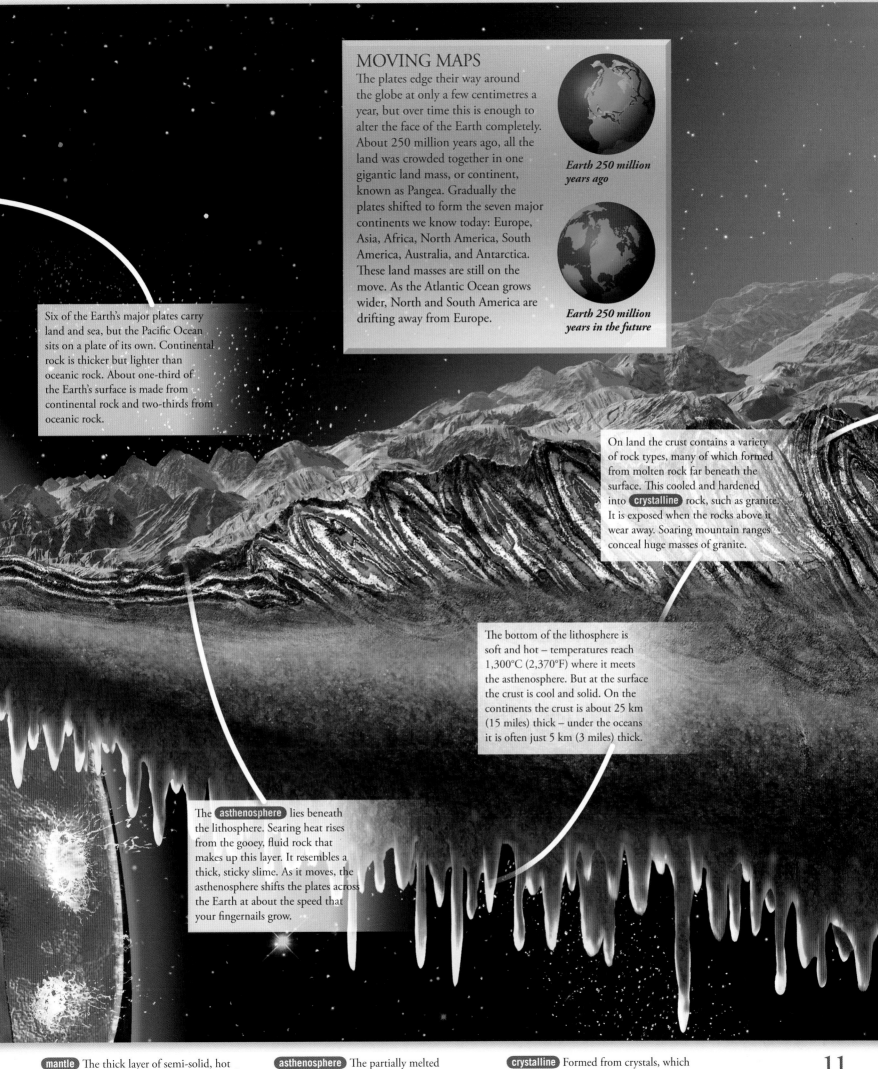

MOVING MAPS

The plates edge their way around the globe at only a few centimetres a year, but over time this is enough to alter the face of the Earth completely. About 250 million years ago, all the land was crowded together in one gigantic land mass, or continent, known as Pangea. Gradually the plates shifted to form the seven major continents we know today: Europe, Asia, Africa, North America, South America, Australia, and Antarctica. These land masses are still on the move. As the Atlantic Ocean grows wider, North and South America are drifting away from Europe.

Earth 250 million years ago

Earth 250 million years in the future

Six of the Earth's major plates carry land and sea, but the Pacific Ocean sits on a plate of its own. Continental rock is thicker but lighter than oceanic rock. About one-third of the Earth's surface is made from continental rock and two-thirds from oceanic rock.

On land the crust contains a variety of rock types, many of which formed from molten rock far beneath the surface. This cooled and hardened into crystalline rock, such as granite. It is exposed when the rocks above it wear away. Soaring mountain ranges conceal huge masses of granite.

The bottom of the lithosphere is soft and hot – temperatures reach 1,300°C (2,370°F) where it meets the asthenosphere. But at the surface the crust is cool and solid. On the continents the crust is about 25 km (15 miles) thick – under the oceans it is often just 5 km (3 miles) thick.

The asthenosphere lies beneath the lithosphere. Searing heat rises from the gooey, fluid rock that makes up this layer. It resembles a thick, sticky slime. As it moves, the asthenosphere shifts the plates across the Earth at about the speed that your fingernails grow.

mantle The thick layer of semi-solid, hot rock between the Earth's core and crust. The upper mantle is fused to the crust.

asthenosphere The partially melted layer of rock that lies beneath the lithosphere.

crystalline Formed from crystals, which are solid minerals with a regular, often symmetrical shape.

DRIFTING

Only 180 million years ago, India was an island off the coast of Australia. As the plates moved, India slowly drifted northeast, squeezing out the ancient Tethys Ocean and eventually crashing into Asia 50 million years ago. This began the mountain-building process that has resulted in the Himalayas.

Indian plate
Eurasian plate

The Himalayas are the tallest mountains in the world – and they are still growing. As India continues its relentless journey northwards, moving at a rate of about 5 cm (2 in) each year, the land continues to fold. The Himalayas grow by about 0.6 cm (¼ in) a year.

Massive mountain ranges are spectacular evidence of continents colliding. The Himalayas in Asia and the Alps in Europe are ranges created by **convergence** – a head-on crash between two plates. As they grind together, the plates crumple and fold to form vast mountains.

SEA ON A MOUNTAIN TOP

On the peaks of some of the highest mountains in the world, including the Himalayas, scientists have found the fossils of sea creatures. This land is now as far from the sea bed as it's possible to get. But some of the rock that is now on peaks and high plateaus once formed the ocean floor. As the plates converged, **sediment** from the bottom of the Tethys Ocean was pushed inland by the Indian plate. Fossils of marine plants and animals are common in Tibet, the high plateau to the north of the Himalayas.

The crust of the land found in the centre of the continents is far older than the ocean crust – some of it is 4 billion years old. The rock that formed the Himalayas is relatively new. Most of it is less than 500 million years old.

Pakicetus is thought to be an early ancestor of the whale, living in sea and on land. Fossils of this creature have been found in the Himalayan region.

Skull and model of a *Pakicetus*

Ammonite

Fossils of ammonites, which are known to have lived in the Tethys Ocean 65 million years ago, have been found high above sea level.

Mountains grow even further underground than they grow above it. Rock is forced downwards by the weight of the mountain above it and the sideways movement of the plates. The roots of the Himalayas are the deepest of any mountains – here, the crust is up to 70 km (45 miles) thick.

convergence When two continental plates push together, forcing the land at the edges to buckle upwards and fold.

sediment Layers of particles, such as discarded shells, sand, and mud, which have been laid down on the ocean floor.

density How compact a substance is. Oceanic rock is thinner but heavier than the thicker but lighter continental rock.

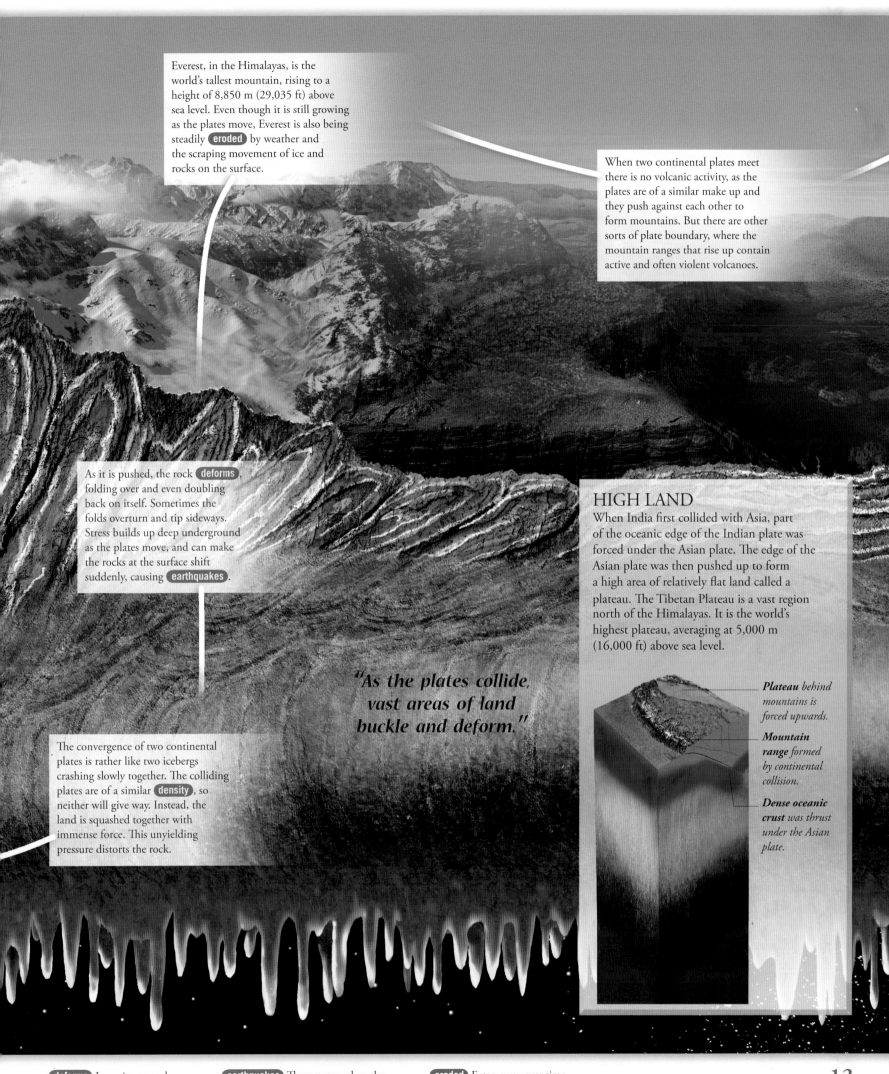

Everest, in the Himalayas, is the world's tallest mountain, rising to a height of 8,850 m (29,035 ft) above sea level. Even though it is still growing as the plates move, Everest is also being steadily **eroded** by weather and the scraping movement of ice and rocks on the surface.

When two continental plates meet there is no volcanic activity, as the plates are of a similar make up and they push against each other to form mountains. But there are other sorts of plate boundary, where the mountain ranges that rise up contain active and often violent volcanoes.

As it is pushed, the rock **deforms**, folding over and even doubling back on itself. Sometimes the folds overturn and tip sideways. Stress builds up deep underground as the plates move, and can make the rocks at the surface shift suddenly, causing **earthquakes**.

HIGH LAND

When India first collided with Asia, part of the oceanic edge of the Indian plate was forced under the Asian plate. The edge of the Asian plate was then pushed up to form a high area of relatively flat land called a plateau. The Tibetan Plateau is a vast region north of the Himalayas. It is the world's highest plateau, averaging at 5,000 m (16,000 ft) above sea level.

"As the plates collide, vast areas of land buckle and deform."

The convergence of two continental plates is rather like two icebergs crashing slowly together. The colliding plates are of a similar **density**, so neither will give way. Instead, the land is squashed together with immense force. This unyielding pressure distorts the rock.

Plateau behind mountains is forced upwards.

***Mountain range** formed by continental collision.*

***Dense oceanic crust** was thrust under the Asian plate.*

deforms Loses its normal shape – flat land becomes squashed and folded.

earthquakes These occur when the plates grind together to create so much stress that the ground cracks and shakes.

eroded Eaten away over time by the forces of weather or moving ice.

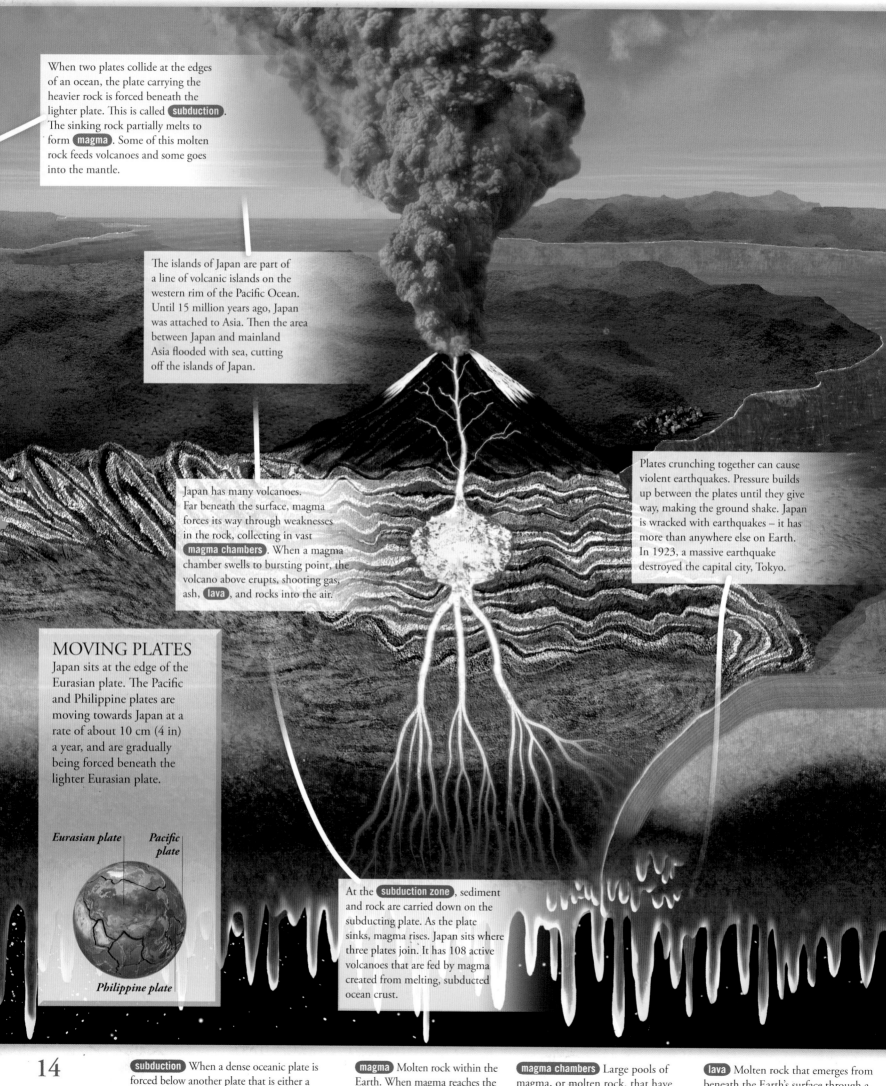

When two plates collide at the edges of an ocean, the plate carrying the heavier rock is forced beneath the lighter plate. This is called **subduction**. The sinking rock partially melts to form **magma**. Some of this molten rock feeds volcanoes and some goes into the mantle.

The islands of Japan are part of a line of volcanic islands on the western rim of the Pacific Ocean. Until 15 million years ago, Japan was attached to Asia. Then the area between Japan and mainland Asia flooded with sea, cutting off the islands of Japan.

Japan has many volcanoes. Far beneath the surface, magma forces its way through weaknesses in the rock, collecting in vast **magma chambers**. When a magma chamber swells to bursting point, the volcano above erupts, shooting gas, ash, **lava**, and rocks into the air.

Plates crunching together can cause violent earthquakes. Pressure builds up between the plates until they give way, making the ground shake. Japan is wracked with earthquakes – it has more than anywhere else on Earth. In 1923, a massive earthquake destroyed the capital city, Tokyo.

MOVING PLATES
Japan sits at the edge of the Eurasian plate. The Pacific and Philippine plates are moving towards Japan at a rate of about 10 cm (4 in) a year, and are gradually being forced beneath the lighter Eurasian plate.

Eurasian plate   *Pacific plate*

Philippine plate

At the **subduction zone**, sediment and rock are carried down on the subducting plate. As the plate sinks, magma rises. Japan sits where three plates join. It has 108 active volcanoes that are fed by magma created from melting, subducted ocean crust.

14

subduction When a dense oceanic plate is forced below another plate that is either a continental plate or a younger oceanic plate.

magma Molten rock within the Earth. When magma reaches the surface it is called lava.

magma chambers Large pools of magma, or molten rock, that have collected beneath the Earth's surface.

lava Molten rock that emerges from beneath the Earth's surface through a crater or a crack in the ground.

RING OF FIRE

Most of the world's volcanoes can be found on the Ring of Fire, a fringe of volcanoes erupting around the edge of the Pacific Ocean. Wherever the Pacific plate meets continental plates or other, younger oceanic plates, subduction feeds volcanoes. Some form arcs of volcanic islands, such as Japan. Others are in mountain ranges formed where the Pacific plate collides with a continent, such as the high peaks of the Andes on the west coast of South America.

Juan de Fuca plate
Eurasian plate
North American plate
RING OF FIRE
Iranian plate
Hawaiian islands
Caribbean plate
Arabian plate
Cocos plate
Somalian sub-plate
Philippine plate
African plate
Australian plate
Pacific plate
Nazca plate
South American plate
Antarctic plate
Andes
Scotia plate

▲ Volcano
— Plate boundary
-- Uncertain plate boundary

Oceanic rock is mostly **basalt**. This is denser and heavier than the rocks found in continental crust, so it sinks further into the soft mantle rock. The low-lying sunken areas flood with water to form seas and oceans. Beneath the cool waters, immense heat is just a few kilometres below.

Where an oceanic plate is forced under a continental plate, a great **oceanic trench** forms. These are the deepest parts of the ocean, plunging to depths of 11 km (7 miles). Trenches are home to creatures that survive in total darkness, extreme cold, and under immense pressure.

DEADLY MOUNTAIN

Mount Fuji is just 90 km (55 miles) southwest of Tokyo. This steep-sided volcano is sacred to the Japanese people. It has erupted 16 times in the past 1,500 years. The last eruption in 1707 spat out 700,000 m³ (25,000,000 cu ft) of lava. The earthquakes that followed triggered massive waves that killed 30,000 people, and the eruption left rice fields barren for 100 years. Tokyo has survived other earthquakes and volcanic activity, but scientists fear Fuji's next eruption is long overdue.

The subducting edge of a plate may be pulled down by gravity. But the plates are also pushed from areas of spreading rock in the middle of the ocean. Here, molten rock wells up from the deeper mantle, forcing the existing rock aside.

subduction zone The area where a denser plate subducts, or is pulled under, another, lighter plate.

oceanic trench A deep depression like a ditch, which is produced by subduction and runs along the ocean floor.

basalt A fine-grained, dark, volcanic rock formed from cooled lava. Most of the rock that forms oceanic crust is basalt.

15

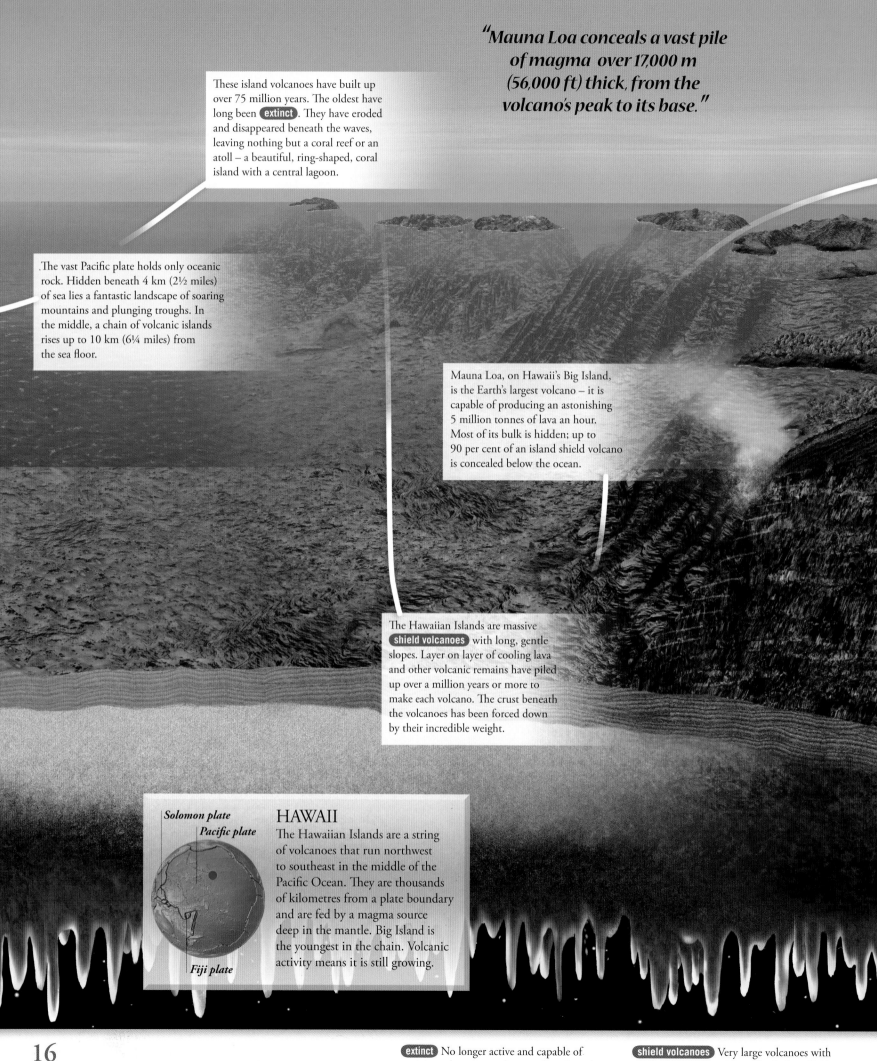

"Mauna Loa conceals a vast pile of magma over 17,000 m (56,000 ft) thick, from the volcano's peak to its base."

These island volcanoes have built up over 75 million years. The oldest have long been **extinct**. They have eroded and disappeared beneath the waves, leaving nothing but a coral reef or an atoll – a beautiful, ring-shaped, coral island with a central lagoon.

The vast Pacific plate holds only oceanic rock. Hidden beneath 4 km (2½ miles) of sea lies a fantastic landscape of soaring mountains and plunging troughs. In the middle, a chain of volcanic islands rises up to 10 km (6¼ miles) from the sea floor.

Mauna Loa, on Hawaii's Big Island, is the Earth's largest volcano – it is capable of producing an astonishing 5 million tonnes of lava an hour. Most of its bulk is hidden; up to 90 per cent of an island shield volcano is concealed below the ocean.

The Hawaiian Islands are massive **shield volcanoes** with long, gentle slopes. Layer on layer of cooling lava and other volcanic remains have piled up over a million years or more to make each volcano. The crust beneath the volcanoes has been forced down by their incredible weight.

Solomon plate
Pacific plate

HAWAII
The Hawaiian Islands are a string of volcanoes that run northwest to southeast in the middle of the Pacific Ocean. They are thousands of kilometres from a plate boundary and are fed by a magma source deep in the mantle. Big Island is the youngest in the chain. Volcanic activity means it is still growing.

Fiji plate

extinct No longer active and capable of erupting – but some volcanoes thought to be extinct burst into life again unexpectedly.

shield volcanoes Very large volcanoes with gently sloping sides that are built from fluid lava rich in basalt.

A long sheet of lava, which looks like a spectacular curtain of fire, is hurled under great pressure from a **fissure** in the ground. These cracks are often ripped open by earthquakes. Kilauea, another volcano on Big Island, has been erupting along an 8-km (5-mile) fissure since 1983.

When lava hits cold sea water, it freezes and instantly shatters into millions of tiny particles. These make up the black sand beaches that are often found on volcanic islands. Hawaii has a unique green sand beach that is made from **olivine** crystals.

HOTSPOTS

Hotspot volcanoes form in the middle of the Earth's plates. Many scientists believe they are formed by a hot plume that rises from deep within the Earth, close to the outer core. The **hotspot** stays in the same place, but the plates move slowly above it. Volcanoes form one after another in a row as the surface above the hotspot moves. The Pacific plate moves across the Hawaiian hotspot at a rate of about 9 cm (3½ in) a year. It has spawned over 200 volcanoes in 75 million years. Many are now extinct and lost beneath the sea.

Magma rising below the surface pools in a huge reservoir 2 km (1½ miles) below the summit of Mauna Loa. This colossal magma chamber holds up to 10 km³ (2½ cu miles) of magma. It also feeds Kilauea, which is one of the most active volcanoes on Earth.

A new volcano, fed by the same plume, is being born under the ocean. In the early stages of this volcano's life, lava squeezes out like toothpaste from a tube, stacking up on the ocean floor. Hawaii's youngest volcano, Loihi, will eventually grow up to form a new island.

The magma wells up from a fountain-like plume deep down in the mantle. This single source supplies several volcanoes through a chain of linked magma chambers. On Big Island, magma flows at a constant rate of 3 m³ (106 cu feet) every second.

fissure A long crack in the ground. Fissures are often opened up by landslips or earthquakes.

olivine A pale-green mineral that is formed from old, eroded basalt lava flows. It is called peridot when used as a gemstone.

hotspot Spot deep within the Earth that feeds magma to the surface, forming chains of hotspot volcanoes, such as Hawaii.

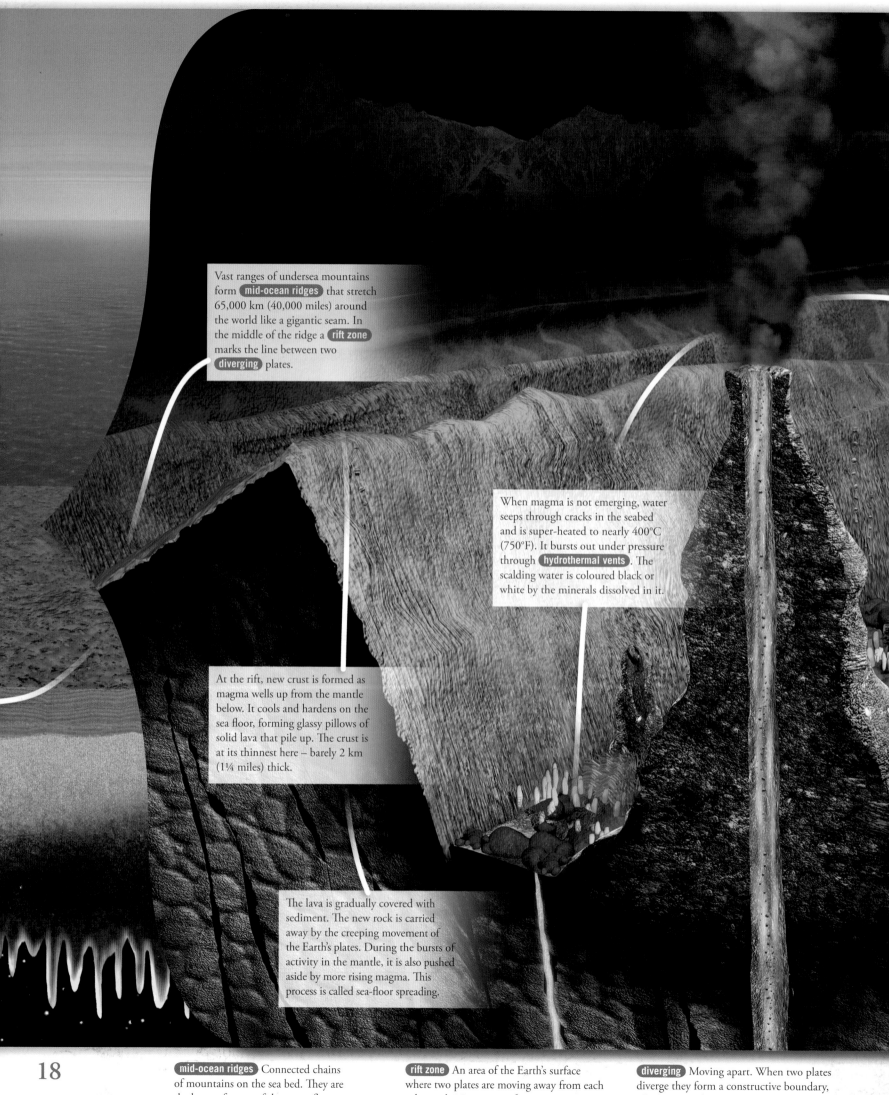

Vast ranges of undersea mountains form **mid-ocean ridges** that stretch 65,000 km (40,000 miles) around the world like a gigantic seam. In the middle of the ridge a **rift zone** marks the line between two **diverging** plates.

When magma is not emerging, water seeps through cracks in the seabed and is super-heated to nearly 400°C (750°F). It bursts out under pressure through **hydrothermal vents**. The scalding water is coloured black or white by the minerals dissolved in it.

At the rift, new crust is formed as magma wells up from the mantle below. It cools and hardens on the sea floor, forming glassy pillows of solid lava that pile up. The crust is at its thinnest here – barely 2 km (1¼ miles) thick.

The lava is gradually covered with sediment. The new rock is carried away by the creeping movement of the Earth's plates. During the bursts of activity in the mantle, it is also pushed aside by more rising magma. This process is called sea-floor spreading.

mid-ocean ridges Connected chains of mountains on the sea bed. They are the largest feature of the ocean floor.

rift zone An area of the Earth's surface where two plates are moving away from each other and rising magma forms new crust.

diverging Moving apart. When two plates diverge they form a constructive boundary, which means that new crust is formed.

JUAN DE FUCA

Pacific plate | *North American plate*

Juan de Fuca plate

The Juan de Fuca plate is a small lithospheric plate that is sandwiched between the Pacific and North American plates. Its boundary with the North American plate is marked by an area of sea-floor spreading, where magma rises to the surface and solidifies to form new crust.

As the minerals solidify in the cooling water, they pile up in tall chimneys called smokers. These can grow several metres in a few months, but they are fragile and easily topple over. The tallest-known black smoker, Godzilla, grew to over 60 m (200 ft).

As it moves away from the rift, the new crust eventually travels towards the subduction zone at the edge of the ocean – a journey that may take 170 million years. The rock will be recycled in the mantle and, after millions more years, it will begin its journey again.

The water from a hydrothermal vent is a poisonous mixture that would kill most sea-life, yet the smokers are home to some of the strangest creatures on Earth. They house tube worms several metres long, glowing crabs, and giant clams the size of dinner plates.

MAPPING THE OCEAN FLOOR

Deep-sea craft and **sonar** map the ocean floor, producing images that reveal an underwater landscape studded with seamounts and plunging ravines. They also show mid-ocean ridges that stretch all around the world, through the Atlantic, Indian, and Pacific Oceans. This false-colour image shows part of the East Pacific Rise, a ridge in the Pacific Ocean.

Seamount, or underwater volcano, forms near ridge.

Crack in the surface separates two parts of the ridge.

Ridge forms above diverging plates.

Beneath the sea floor, magma leaks through cracks leading up from a shallow magma chamber and oozes from crevices at the surface. It takes 150–200 million years to renew the entire ocean floor. New crust forms at a rate of up to 20 cm (8 in) a year.

hydrothermal vents Cracks in the Earth through which super-heated water spurts under huge pressure.

sonar Using beams of sound and their echoes to measure the depth of the ocean and locate objects on the sea floor.

19

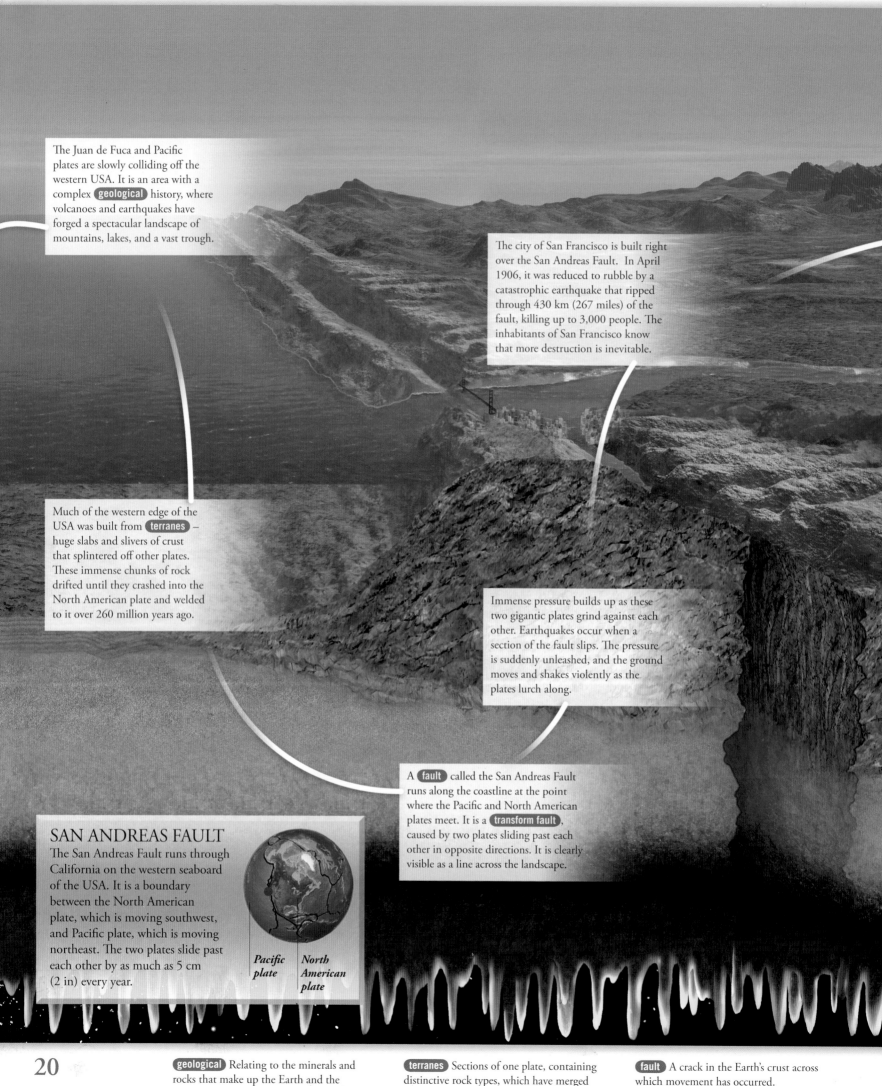

The Juan de Fuca and Pacific plates are slowly colliding off the western USA. It is an area with a complex **geological** history, where volcanoes and earthquakes have forged a spectacular landscape of mountains, lakes, and a vast trough.

The city of San Francisco is built right over the San Andreas Fault. In April 1906, it was reduced to rubble by a catastrophic earthquake that ripped through 430 km (267 miles) of the fault, killing up to 3,000 people. The inhabitants of San Francisco know that more destruction is inevitable.

Much of the western edge of the USA was built from **terranes** – huge slabs and slivers of crust that splintered off other plates. These immense chunks of rock drifted until they crashed into the North American plate and welded to it over 260 million years ago.

Immense pressure builds up as these two gigantic plates grind against each other. Earthquakes occur when a section of the fault slips. The pressure is suddenly unleashed, and the ground moves and shakes violently as the plates lurch along.

A **fault** called the San Andreas Fault runs along the coastline at the point where the Pacific and North American plates meet. It is a **transform fault**, caused by two plates sliding past each other in opposite directions. It is clearly visible as a line across the landscape.

SAN ANDREAS FAULT

The San Andreas Fault runs through California on the western seaboard of the USA. It is a boundary between the North American plate, which is moving southwest, and Pacific plate, which is moving northeast. The two plates slide past each other by as much as 5 cm (2 in) every year.

Pacific plate   *North American plate*

geological Relating to the minerals and rocks that make up the Earth and the processes that have formed it.

terranes Sections of one plate, containing distinctive rock types, which have merged with a plate of a different make up.

fault A crack in the Earth's crust across which movement has occurred.

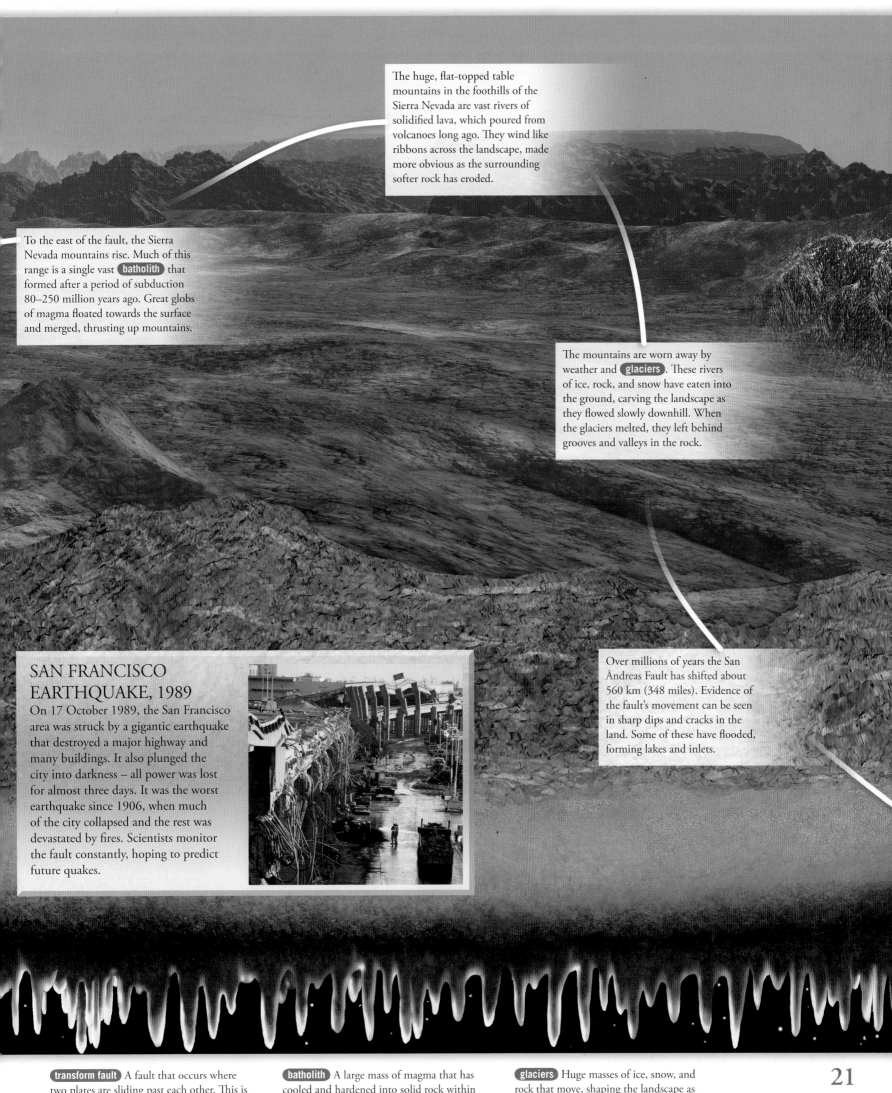

The huge, flat-topped table mountains in the foothills of the Sierra Nevada are vast rivers of solidified lava, which poured from volcanoes long ago. They wind like ribbons across the landscape, made more obvious as the surrounding softer rock has eroded.

To the east of the fault, the Sierra Nevada mountains rise. Much of this range is a single vast **batholith** that formed after a period of subduction 80–250 million years ago. Great globs of magma floated towards the surface and merged, thrusting up mountains.

The mountains are worn away by weather and **glaciers**. These rivers of ice, rock, and snow have eaten into the ground, carving the landscape as they flowed slowly downhill. When the glaciers melted, they left behind grooves and valleys in the rock.

SAN FRANCISCO EARTHQUAKE, 1989

On 17 October 1989, the San Francisco area was struck by a gigantic earthquake that destroyed a major highway and many buildings. It also plunged the city into darkness – all power was lost for almost three days. It was the worst earthquake since 1906, when much of the city collapsed and the rest was devastated by fires. Scientists monitor the fault constantly, hoping to predict future quakes.

Over millions of years the San Andreas Fault has shifted about 560 km (348 miles). Evidence of the fault's movement can be seen in sharp dips and cracks in the land. Some of these have flooded, forming lakes and inlets.

transform fault A fault that occurs where two plates are sliding past each other. This is sometimes called a conservative fault.

batholith A large mass of magma that has cooled and hardened into solid rock within the Earth's crust.

glaciers Huge masses of ice, snow, and rock that move, shaping the landscape as they do so.

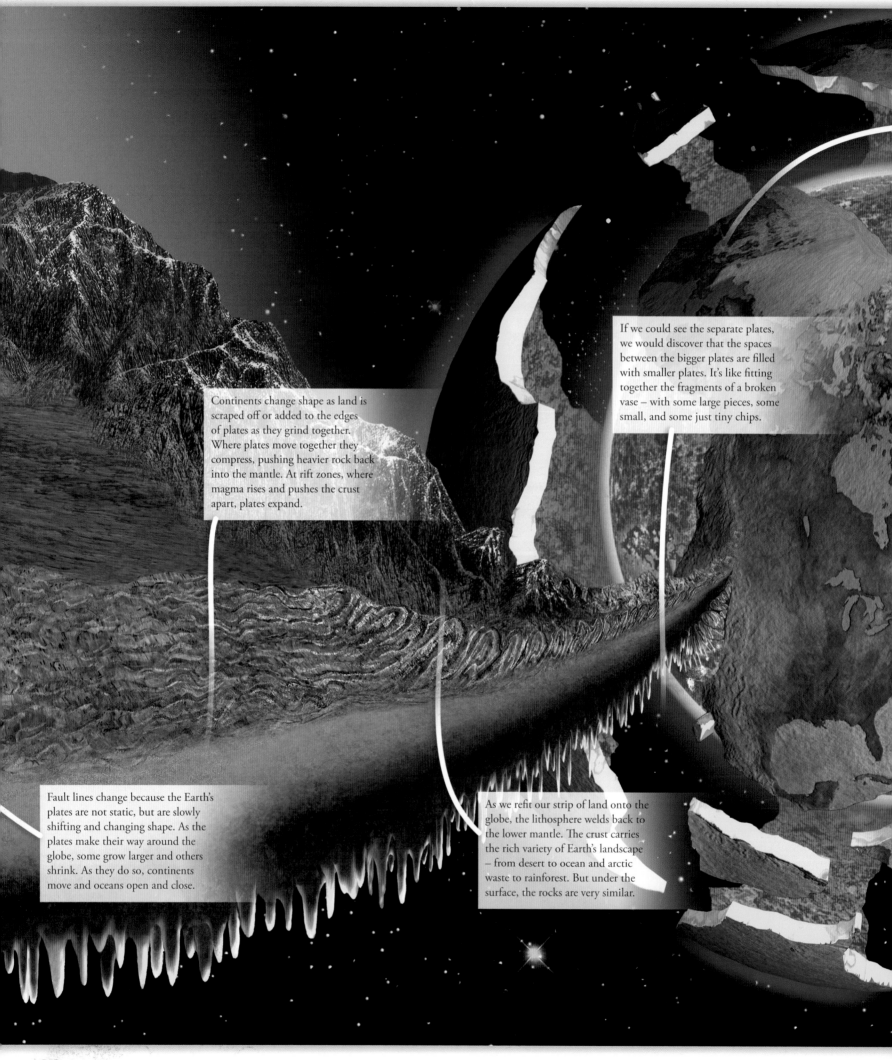

If we could see the separate plates, we would discover that the spaces between the bigger plates are filled with smaller plates. It's like fitting together the fragments of a broken vase – with some large pieces, some small, and some just tiny chips.

Continents change shape as land is scraped off or added to the edges of plates as they grind together. Where plates move together they compress, pushing heavier rock back into the mantle. At rift zones, where magma rises and pushes the crust apart, plates expand.

Fault lines change because the Earth's plates are not static, but are slowly shifting and changing shape. As the plates make their way around the globe, some grow larger and others shrink. As they do so, continents move and oceans open and close.

As we refit our strip of land onto the globe, the lithosphere welds back to the lower mantle. The crust carries the rich variety of Earth's landscape – from desert to ocean and arctic waste to rainforest. But under the surface, the rocks are very similar.

The continental plates are more deeply rooted in the Earth and move more slowly than the oceanic plates. The crust beneath the Himalayas has the deepest roots, and moves most slowly of all – about 2 cm (¾ in) a year.

Movement is not just across the surface. Some regions are sinking into the mantle. Land weighed down by a blanket of ice during the last **ice age** is slowly bobbing back up – eastern Canada and Greenland are rising about 12 mm (½ in) a year.

Although the process is incredibly slow, the movement of the plates is still rearranging the continents and seas and forging new mountains and volcanoes. If we could visit Earth millions of years in the future, this map would be unrecognizable.

THE EARTH'S PLATES

The seven largest plates, from biggest to smallest, are the Pacific, African, Eurasian, Australian, North American, Antarctic, and South American plates, which together cover more than 90 percent of the globe. Most of the plates are a mixture of oceanic and continental rock, but the Pacific is entirely oceanic.

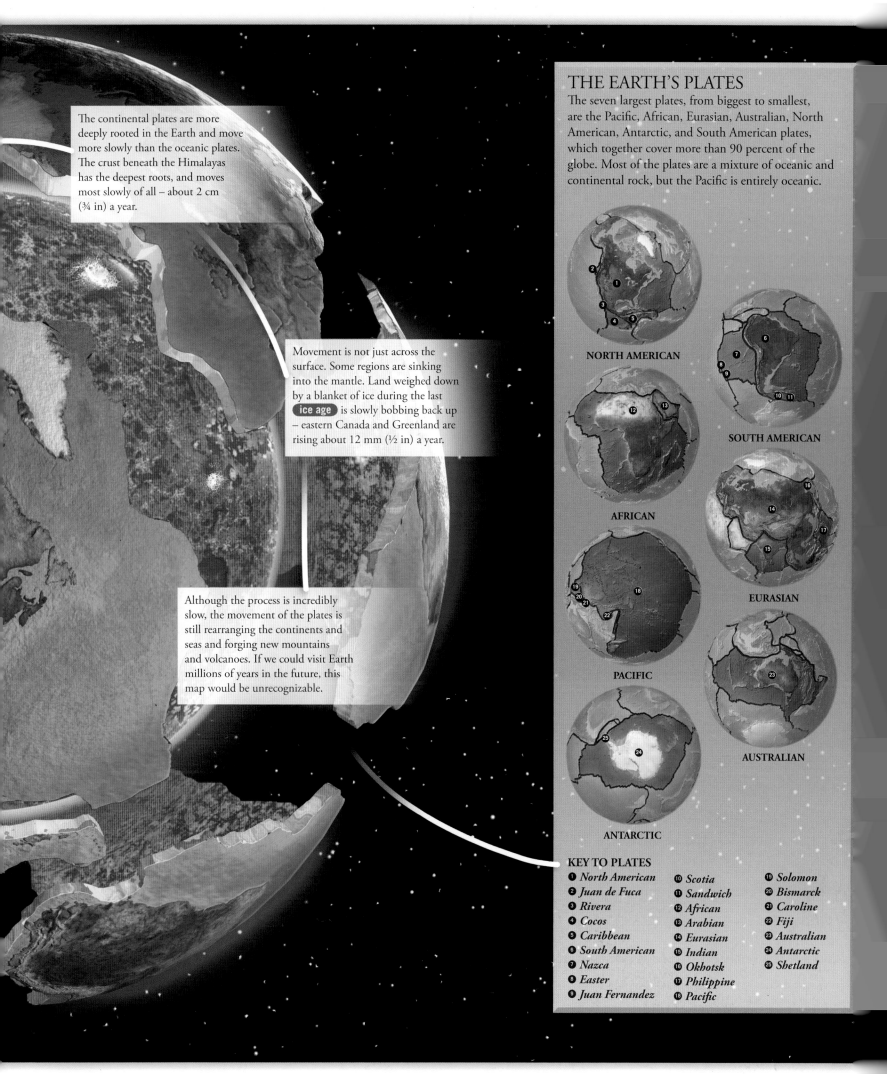

NORTH AMERICAN

SOUTH AMERICAN

AFRICAN

EURASIAN

PACIFIC

AUSTRALIAN

ANTARCTIC

KEY TO PLATES

❶ North American
❷ Juan de Fuca
❸ Rivera
❹ Cocos
❺ Caribbean
❻ South American
❼ Nazca
❽ Easter
❾ Juan Fernandez
❿ Scotia
⓫ Sandwich
⓬ African
⓭ Arabian
⓮ Eurasian
⓯ Indian
⓰ Okhotsk
⓱ Philippine
⓲ Pacific
⓳ Solomon
⓴ Bismarck
㉑ Caroline
㉒ Fiji
㉓ Australian
㉔ Antarctic
㉕ Shetland

ice age A period in the Earth's history when ice covered much of the globe. The last ice age ended about 10,000 years ago.

PELEE

ENGULFED BY A FIRESTORM

In two terrible minutes, the population of St-Pierre on the beautiful Caribbean island of Martinique was wiped out. The mountain towering over the city exploded, wreaking havoc that turned their idyllic island first to a scorching furnace and then to a barren wasteland.

Fire mountain

Martinique, known as the "Pearl of the Caribbean", made its money from rum distilleries and sugar production. Local people called the pale green peak on the horizon "Fire Mountain", but it had been largely peaceful for 300 years. In 1902, it woke from its long sleep. After minor earthquakes and the appearance of holes belching sulphurous fumes, an explosion of steam, ash, and dust startled the inhabitants on 24 April.

The volcano stirs

In May, explosions, ash falls, and a catastrophic mudflow gave a clear and frightening signal. The mountain released columns of steam and gas into the air and hurled out huge globs of semi-molten rock. Lightning flickered through the column of smoke and deafening bangs shook the area. Poisonous snakes, giant centipedes, and insects fled the mountain, infesting towns and villages and biting people and their animals. At least 50 people died of snake bites.

Fear and panic

The authorities tried to calm the island's terrified residents. Those who lived on the slopes moved downhill to St-Pierre, hoping to be safe from any lava flow. This boosted its population by about 2,000 to more than 27,000. On the night of 7 May, a fierce storm added to the chaos. Many demanded the last rites from priests, convinced they were about to die.

This news photograph, taken not long after the blast in 1902, shows two visitors picking their way through St-Pierre's ruined streets. Few buildings escaped unscathed – most were reduced to roofless shells or piles of rubble.

"I prayed with my crucifix in my hand and expected death at any moment."

Emilie Dujon, who fled with her household from Le Prêcheur to St-Pierre to escape the choking ash

In this dramatic painting, *rescuers arriving at St-Pierre by boat discover a scene of total devastation.*

PELEE TIMELINE

March–April 1902 A powerful smell of rotten eggs comes from new holes opening in Mount Pelée.
24 April Steam, ash, and dust pour from the volcano.
25 April After a big explosion, rocks hurtle into the air.

1 May Loud bangs wake people in the town of Le Prêcheur; by afternoon, it is so dark that lamps are lit.
2 May, 11.00 pm A column of ash and gas, laced with lightning, rises 3 km (2 miles) above the mountain.

5 May The rim of the crater gives way, releasing water from the crater lake to make a deadly mudflow.
8 May, dawn Dark clouds of ash darken the sky and shoot beyond the city of St-Pierre to fall into the sea.

Now green and peaceful, Mount Pelée still looms over St-Pierre and its sheltered bay. The city never regained its former glory, and is now a tourist resort.

Glowing cloud

The cataclysm came in the early morning of 8 May, but it took a form no-one expected. The volcano shuddered and seemed to tear apart, then sent a fiery cloud roaring down the mountainside, engulfing St-Pierre within seconds. People died where they stood, never knowing what happened. It took only two or three minutes for the terrible cloud to tear through the city. Immediately following it, a firestorm fuelled by the wind and casks of rum raged through the ruins of the city at temperatures of up to 900°C (1,650°F), scorching everything in its path. In the entire centre of the city, there were just two survivors. On the edges of the area caught by the burning cloud, there were a few more survivors, though many were horribly injured by breathing in the scalding air. It was the worst volcanic disaster since the destruction of Pompeii in AD 79, and had the same cause. Scientists studying

Two bodies lie face down in volcanic slurry, having been trapped by a terrifying mudflow.

the eruption of Mount Pelée named the phenomenon a *nuée ardente* (glowing cloud).

Aftermath

When officials in nearby towns heard nothing from St-Pierre all morning, they became alarmed. Boats were sent to investigate, but returned with awful stories of a demolished city, the inhabitants all dead, the land still too hot for anyone to land. People with friends and relatives in

> "He had just finished his sentence when I heard a dreadful scream, then another much weaker groan, like a stifled death rattle. Then silence."
>
> *A businessman who had been on the phone to a friend in St-Pierre at 8.02 am on 8 May*

One of only two survivors was 25-year-old Louis-Auguste Sylbaris, who later joined a circus. Posters advertising his act boasted that he had survived the "silent city of death".

St-Pierre crowded the quays, desperately hoping for news of survivors. None came.

Second explosion

The volcano had not finished. Another *nuée ardente* swept through St-Pierre on 30 August. Now, though, there were only a few looters in the city – they met a grisly fate. The mountain remained active for months, and many more fiery winds rolled down its slopes until the middle of 1903.

Devastating facts

The Plinian-style eruption of Mount Pelée was the most destructive of the 20th century. In barely two minutes, 27,000 people lost their lives in the first recorded *nuée ardente*, or "glowing cloud".

Deafening roar	People heard the eruption in Venezuela, South America, 4,680 km (2,910 miles) away.
Terrible toll	The eruption killed about 27,000 people and left another 25,000 homeless.
Scorching wind	The searing blast of the *nuée ardente* raced down the volcano at 500 km/h (310 mph) and at temperatures of 200–450°C (390–840°F).
Hot as a furnace	A firestorm started by the *nuée ardente* was fuelled by St-Pierre's massive stores of rum. During the storm, the air became even hotter than rocks leaving the volcano's crater.
And again	On 30 August a powerful second *nuée ardente* covered twice the area of the first.
Lucky survivor	Louis-Auguste Sylbaris, a prisoner in jail behind thick stone walls, was rescued from the wreckage of St-Pierre after three days.
Strange structure	After the eruption, a spectacular column of lava nicknamed "The Needle of Pelée" grew from the volcano's crater. It was unlike anything seen before, but eventually toppled in March 1903 when 230 m (755 ft) high.

8.02 am A telegraph message is cut off after a few seconds, indicating the exact time of St-Pierre's destruction.
8.05 am Fast-moving cloud of hot gases incinerates the city – virtually all its residents perish.

12.30 pm A steamship carries news of the disaster to Martinique's capital, Fort-de-France.
30 August Second burning gas cloud kills 1,000 people.
1 September Mount Pelée releases third deadly gas cloud.

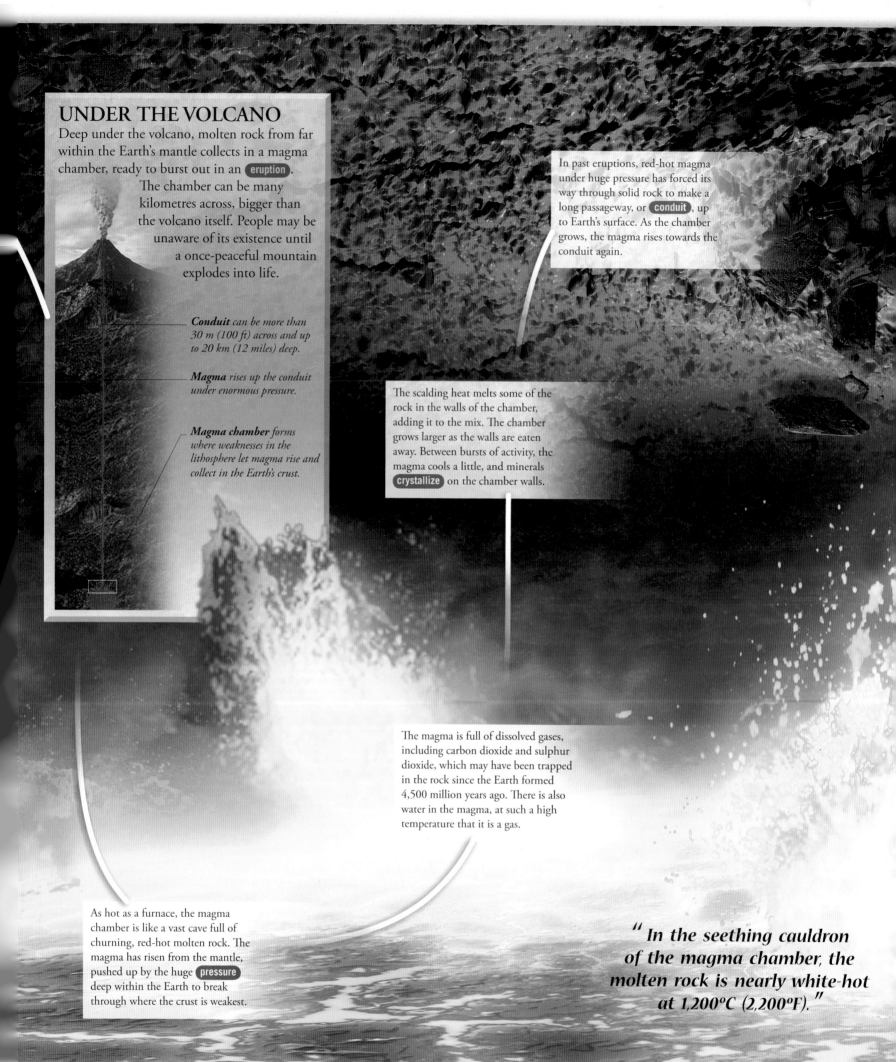

UNDER THE VOLCANO

Deep under the volcano, molten rock from far within the Earth's mantle collects in a magma chamber, ready to burst out in an `eruption`. The chamber can be many kilometres across, bigger than the volcano itself. People may be unaware of its existence until a once-peaceful mountain explodes into life.

Conduit *can be more than 30 m (100 ft) across and up to 20 km (12 miles) deep.*

Magma *rises up the conduit under enormous pressure.*

Magma chamber *forms where weaknesses in the lithosphere let magma rise and collect in the Earth's crust.*

In past eruptions, red-hot magma under huge pressure has forced its way through solid rock to make a long passageway, or `conduit`, up to Earth's surface. As the chamber grows, the magma rises towards the conduit again.

The scalding heat melts some of the rock in the walls of the chamber, adding it to the mix. The chamber grows larger as the walls are eaten away. Between bursts of activity, the magma cools a little, and minerals `crystallize` on the chamber walls.

The magma is full of dissolved gases, including carbon dioxide and sulphur dioxide, which may have been trapped in the rock since the Earth formed 4,500 million years ago. There is also water in the magma, at such a high temperature that it is a gas.

As hot as a furnace, the magma chamber is like a vast cave full of churning, red-hot molten rock. The magma has risen from the mantle, pushed up by the huge `pressure` deep within the Earth to break through where the crust is weakest.

" In the seething cauldron of the magma chamber, the molten rock is nearly white-hot at 1,200°C (2,200°F). "

`eruption` Explosion of hot magma, rocks, gases, steam, and ash (any or all of these) from a volcano.

`pressure` Force produced by a solid, liquid, or gas pressing on something. Pressure inside the Earth increases towards the centre.

`crystallize` Cool and harden to make crystals. Many of the minerals that build rocks and precious gems are formed from crystals.

As more and more magma rises from deep in the Earth, the chamber expands with the heat and the enormous pressure. Above ground, the mountain may swell or bulge. The chamber can even explode, blowing the mountain apart.

Magma leaks into the surrounding rock through cracks and weaknesses in the chamber walls. Scorching magma may seep through to the surface as well as bursting from the mouth of the volcano, or it may cool and harden below the surface.

The magma chamber is filled to bursting point, as the pressure inside it soars. The surrounding rock can no longer hold the magma, which has to escape. It bursts into the conduit to start its upward journey of many kilometres to the Earth's surface.

Magma can be as runny as honey or more **viscous** than peanut butter. Extra **silica** dissolving from the walls of the chamber changes the magma, making it even more sticky. Viscous magma with a lot of gas makes the most dangerous eruptions.

The magma nearest the top of the chamber is lighter and contains most gas. This will rush up the conduit first, giving the eruption an explosive start. Thicker, less gassy magma will follow later, and emerge more slowly from the volcano.

Although the magma is incredibly hot, water and gas cannot escape from the mixture because they are held in by the huge pressure in the chamber. It is like shaking a bottle of fizzy drink – bubbles do not appear until the cap is taken off, letting the pressure drop.

conduit Passageway that links the magma chamber with the mouth of the volcano above.

viscous Thick or runny. The less viscous a liquid is, the more easily it flows.

silica Silicon dioxide, the most common mineral found in the Earth's crust.

TYPES OF LAVA

When magma escapes from a volcano, it is called lava. Most lavas are made from different amounts of the same minerals. The most important of these is silica. The way in which the lava erupts depends on how the magma builds up within the volcano. Thin, runny lava may spurt far into the air if it carries a lot of gas, spattering and spraying in great fountains. Thin lava with less gas runs quickly and evenly down a mountain or forms lava lakes. Thick lava with lots of gas may explode from a volcano, but if it contains little gas, it oozes out and slides down the slope or piles up.

A'a lava

A thick, slowly moving pile of crispy lava edges its way along the ground. It will harden to a crunchy mass of sharp, brittle rock. This huge mass pushes hardened chunks of rock before it, making a clinking sound.

Flow thickness: 2–20 m (6½–65 ft)
Gas content: High
Viscosity: High
Silica content: Medium

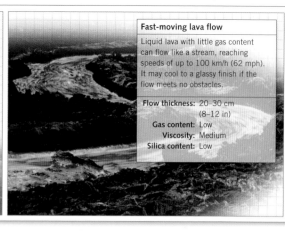

Fast-moving lava flow

Liquid lava with little gas content can flow like a stream, reaching speeds of up to 100 km/h (62 mph). It may cool to a glassy finish if the flow meets no obstacles.

Flow thickness: 20–30 cm (8–12 in)
Gas content: Low
Viscosity: Medium
Silica content: Low

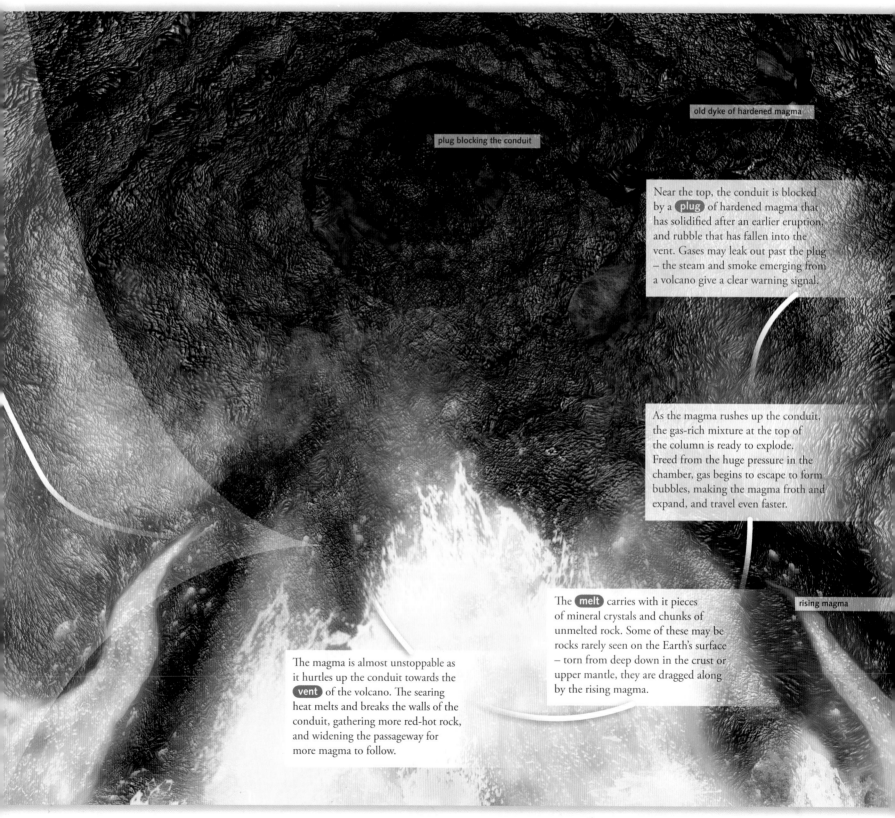

old dyke of hardened magma

plug blocking the conduit

Near the top, the conduit is blocked by a **plug** of hardened magma that has solidified after an earlier eruption, and rubble that has fallen into the vent. Gases may leak out past the plug – the steam and smoke emerging from a volcano give a clear warning signal.

As the magma rushes up the conduit, the gas-rich mixture at the top of the column is ready to explode. Freed from the huge pressure in the chamber, gas begins to escape to form bubbles, making the magma froth and expand, and travel even faster.

The **melt** carries with it pieces of mineral crystals and chunks of unmelted rock. Some of these may be rocks rarely seen on the Earth's surface – torn from deep down in the crust or upper mantle, they are dragged along by the rising magma.

rising magma

The magma is almost unstoppable as it hurtles up the conduit towards the **vent** of the volcano. The searing heat melts and breaks the walls of the conduit, gathering more red-hot rock, and widening the passageway for more magma to follow.

vent Opening where gases and magma can escape into the air.

melt Mixture of molten rock with dissolved gases, water, and chunks of solid rock, that forms magma.

plug Blockage made of hardened magma, rubble, and debris in the conduit.

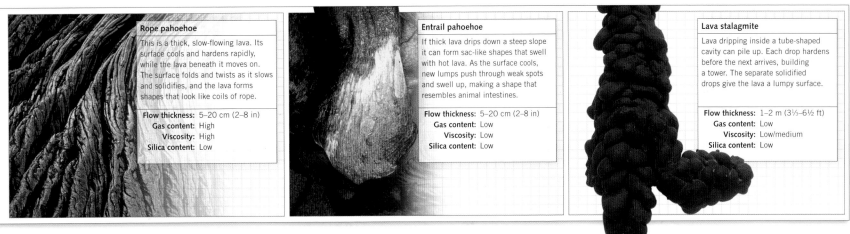

Rope pahoehoe

This is a thick, slow-flowing lava. Its surface cools and hardens rapidly, while the lava beneath it moves on. The surface folds and twists as it slows, and the lava forms shapes that look like coils of rope.

Flow thickness: 5–20 cm (2–8 in)
Gas content: High
Viscosity: High
Silica content: Low

Entrail pahoehoe

If thick lava drips down a steep slope it can form sac-like shapes that swell with hot lava. As the surface cools, new lumps push through weak spots and swell up, making a shape that resembles animal intestines.

Flow thickness: 5–20 cm (2–8 in)
Gas content: Low
Viscosity: Low
Silica content: Low

Lava stalagmite

Lava dripping inside a tube-shaped cavity can pile up. Each drop hardens before the next arrives, building a tower. The separate solidified drops give the lava a lumpy surface.

Flow thickness: 1–2 m (3⅓–6½ ft)
Gas content: Low
Viscosity: Low/medium
Silica content: Low

cone of the volcano

plug of solid magma

Some magma is squeezed from the conduit into branching **dykes** that carry it off underground, or into the flanks of the mountain. Most of the magma continues to gush upwards, hitting the plug with tremendous force, and exploding it.

magma rises in conduit

magma flows into dykes

remnants of the plug

vent fills with magma

magma flows into dykes

layers of ash and rock

The magma continues to smash its way along the conduit, shattering or melting the plug as it goes. Further dykes open up in the layers of ash and rock that form the **cone**. Finally, the magma reaches the vent, and all that remains above it is a thin crust.

dykes Rock formations that occur when magma invades a vertical fissure, or crack. The magma then cools and solidifies.

cone Cone-shaped hill or mountain of volcanic material, built up by one eruption after another.

29

"The volcano is ready to hurl several cubic kilometres of red-hot liquid rock far into the air."

The rim of the crater and the top of the cone are bare, black rock. Searing heat and **toxic** volcanic gases, such as sulphur dioxide and carbon dioxide, have killed all the grass and other plants, leaving a barren, alien landscape, where nothing can survive.

The wall of the crater reveals the volcano's turbulent history. The evidence of past eruptions can be clearly seen in the layers of **compacted**, hardened ash and lava that have erupted and built up the cone over many thousands of years.

The walls of the crater are heated to red-hot by the scorching magma. Chunks may crumble and fall off, mixing into the melt and widening the crater. If the crater walls are breached, lava will pour down the mountainside.

In the last moments before the eruption, the rising magma finally breaks through the remaining crust of rock separating it from the outside world. The **crater** of the volcano is a seething mass of fiery, molten rock about to explode into the air.

The magma in the crater heaves and churns as bubbles burst and release scalding gas. The surface may rise and fall by as much as 6 m (20 ft). It spits and hisses as gas escapes, spattering hot lava high into the air. The volcano may even boom and roar.

crater Steep-sided hollow formed at the Earth's surface, where lava spills out of the vent.

toxic Poisonous.

compacted Pressed down and packed together.

VOLCANO LEGENDS

Scientists can now explain volcanoes by studying what happens inside the Earth, but for thousands of years many cultures have developed stories to explain why some mountains explode. Some people still believe that the Hawaiian goddess of fire, Pele, lives in the volcano Kilauea, and prayers are still said to her to stop lava flows from destroying houses. In Roman times, Vulcan, blacksmith of the gods, sent out fiery sparks from his forge under the Italian island of Vulcano. And, according to Maori legend, the volcanoes around Lake Taupo in New Zealand were powerful giants, who fought for the love of a female mountain, hurling fire and rocks at each other.

PELE, GODDESS OF FIRE

Clouds of gas and steam pour out – a poisonous, acidic mix, at a searing temperature. The wind can sometimes carry the deadly fumes downhill, killing livestock, crops, and even people, and enveloping the land in a toxic fog that can last for weeks.

Red-hot rock begins to break through parts of the mountainside as magma rises towards the surface. The ground softens, bulges, and becomes unstable, or splits as liquid lava forces its way through from beneath. The pressure inside the volcano is immense.

From the side of the volcano, **fumaroles** leak blisteringly hot gas and steam. Sulphur and other minerals crystallized from the gases build up around the rocky edges of the fumaroles, leaving a yellow crust – a tell-tale sign of volcanic activity.

fumaroles Holes in the surface of the Earth through which volcanic gases and steam pour out.

31

At last, the pressure becomes so intense that the volcano erupts with a deafening explosion, shooting out a **plume** of lava, **ash**, and gas. In a big eruption, ash and gas can be blasted 30 km (19 miles) upwards in only 10 minutes, darkening the sky.

The volume of the water in the rising magma increases a thousand fold as it turns to steam, and blows apart the magma, turning it to ash. Now a **suspension** of ash and lava particles held in gas, the plume can travel from the conduit as fast as a supersonic jet.

A fiery fountain of lava, gas, and ash shoots up from the crater in a spectacular but deadly display. The lava rushing from the vent scours, melts, and widens the mouth of the volcano, making the eruption even more violent.

Lava spills from the crater at 1,200°C (2,200°F). It stays molten long enough to flow several kilometres, scorching a path on its way down the mountainside. Runny lava can begin its journey at speeds of up to 60 km/h (37 mph), but it slows as it cools.

plume A rising column of material, such as volcanic ash and gas.

ash Very fine, hard particles of shattered lava, measuring less than 2 mm (¹⁄₁₀ in). It is grey or whitish in colour.

suspension Mixture of particles held in a gas or liquid.

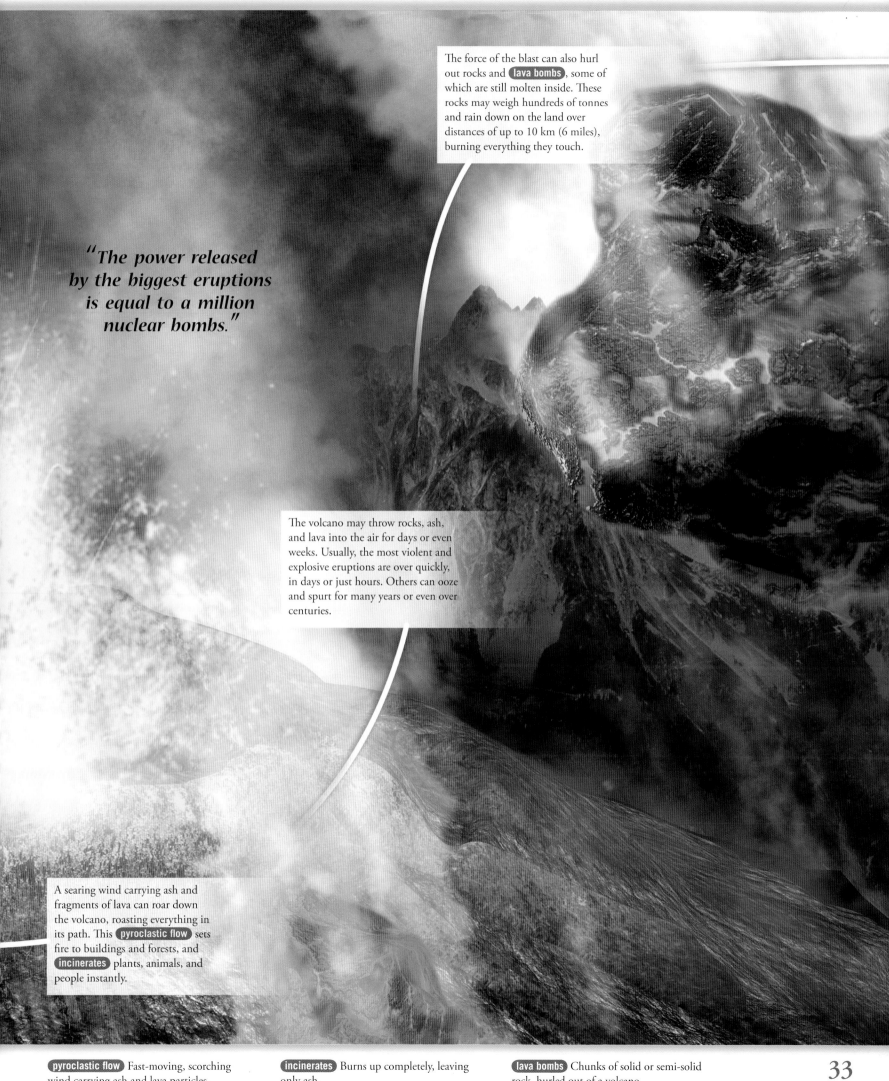

The force of the blast can also hurl out rocks and **lava bombs**, some of which are still molten inside. These rocks may weigh hundreds of tonnes and rain down on the land over distances of up to 10 km (6 miles), burning everything they touch.

"The power released by the biggest eruptions is equal to a million nuclear bombs."

The volcano may throw rocks, ash, and lava into the air for days or even weeks. Usually, the most violent and explosive eruptions are over quickly, in days or just hours. Others can ooze and spurt for many years or even over centuries.

A searing wind carrying ash and fragments of lava can roar down the volcano, roasting everything in its path. This **pyroclastic flow** sets fire to buildings and forests, and **incinerates** plants, animals, and people instantly.

pyroclastic flow Fast-moving, scorching wind carrying ash and lava particles.

incinerates Burns up completely, leaving only ash.

lava bombs Chunks of solid or semi-solid rock, hurled out of a volcano.

33

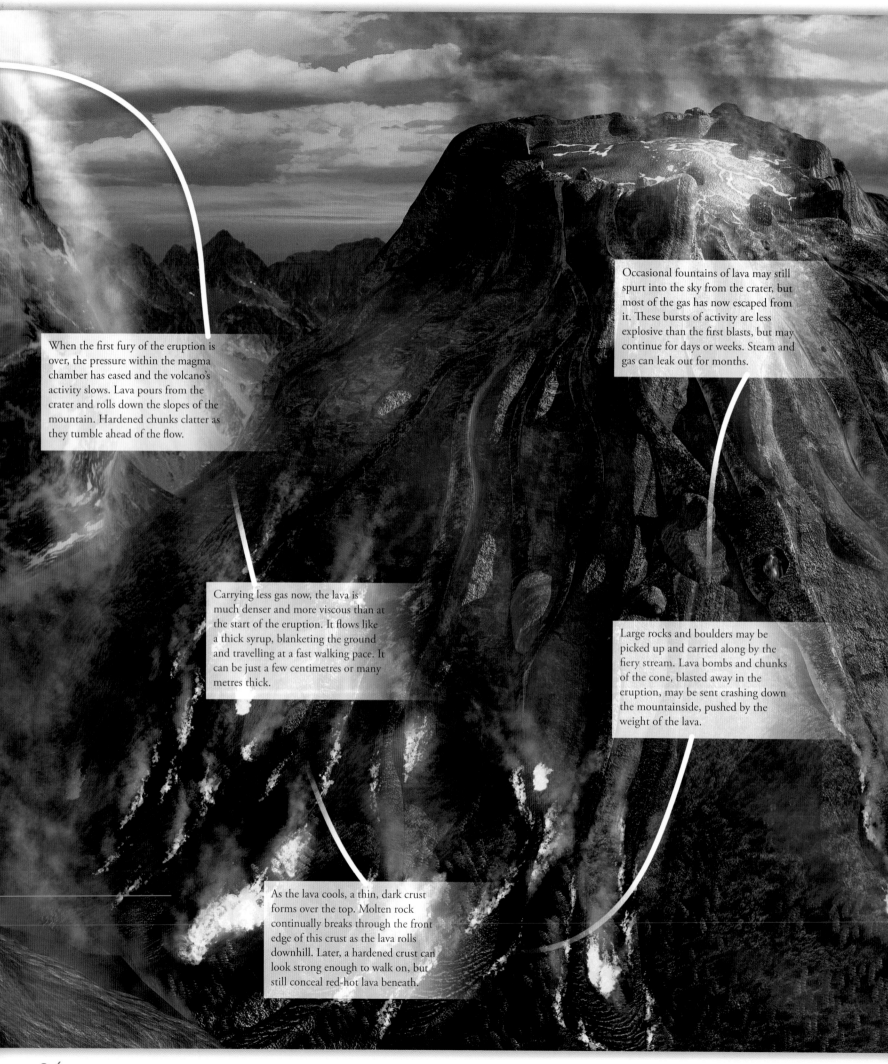

When the first fury of the eruption is over, the pressure within the magma chamber has eased and the volcano's activity slows. Lava pours from the crater and rolls down the slopes of the mountain. Hardened chunks clatter as they tumble ahead of the flow.

Occasional fountains of lava may still spurt into the sky from the crater, but most of the gas has now escaped from it. These bursts of activity are less explosive than the first blasts, but may continue for days or weeks. Steam and gas can leak out for months.

Carrying less gas now, the lava is much denser and more viscous than at the start of the eruption. It flows like a thick syrup, blanketing the ground and travelling at a fast walking pace. It can be just a few centimetres or many metres thick.

Large rocks and boulders may be picked up and carried along by the fiery stream. Lava bombs and chunks of the cone, blasted away in the eruption, may be sent crashing down the mountainside, pushed by the weight of the lava.

As the lava cools, a thin, dark crust forms over the top. Molten rock continually breaks through the front edge of this crust as the lava rolls downhill. Later, a hardened crust can look strong enough to walk on, but still conceal red-hot lava beneath.

SAVING THE DAY

For thousands of years, people have courted danger to farm fertile volcanic soil. When disaster threatens, they have tried to avert it by steering lava flows away from towns, villages, and important buildings. The use of prayers, charms, and sacrifices has not been able to prevent casualties. But technology, ranging from primitive barriers to modern ditches, dams, and carefully engineered concrete walls, has had only limited success.

Whatever the flowing lava touches, it burns. Buildings and trees burst into flames and are pushed over by its relentless force. Only seeds and animals hidden deep underground survive the onslaught of heat, ash, and lava, to reappear after the devastation.

Where the lava burns green vegetation , a gas is produced, which collects in pockets and cracks underground. This methane gas can catch fire, causing sudden explosions that throw earth, rocks, and vegetation several metres into the air.

If lava rolls into the sea or a lake, huge clouds of steam hiss and spurt up as the hot lava boils the water. The lava cools instantly and fragments, exploding into razor-sharp shards of volcanic glass that form part of the black sand on volcanic beaches.

vegetation Trees, grass and all other types of plants.

methane Gas composed of hydrogen and carbon, that burns very easily.

shards Slivers or fragments of sharp rock or glass. As shards break from newly cooled lava, they may produce a tinkling sound.

The violence of the eruption subsides when magma is no longer forced upwards from the chamber below. A changed landscape is revealed – blackened, lifeless, and quite alien. The cone may have collapsed, the top of the volcano crashing downwards into its magma chamber.

Some red-hot lava may still escape from fissures. With little gas remaining, and little pressure forcing it outwards, the lava oozes slowly now. It is quite different from the spurting, gas-filled orange fountains of the eruption's early stages.

LAVA TUBES

Lava tubes form when the surface of hot lava, flowing in a channel, hardens into a roof and encloses it, making a tube. The lava is kept hot by the insulating rock that surrounds it and can run through hidden tubes for up to 80 km (50 miles), unseen from above. When the lava stops flowing and finally runs out, the empty tube is left underground.

Glassy, flat grey layers appear where a flow of runny **pahoehoe** lava, containing little gas, has cooled quickly. The newly hardened surface of the flow forms a thin skin, which is stretched and split by hot lava expanding it from beneath, leaving it laced with cracks.

36

pahoehoe A Hawaiian word that describes a smooth, slow-flowing lava, which may form a wrinkly or smooth skin as it cools.

The air is hot and difficult to breathe, because it is choked with ash and sulphur fumes. After a major eruption, fine ash can be carried all around the world by winds. If it remains high in the atmosphere, it can create dramatic sunrises and sunsets long after the volcano has fallen silent.

Layers of ash and tephra may cover the landscape for miles around after a large eruption. These layers, laid down by repeated eruptions, are slowly pressed together, forming the rock of the volcano itself. The scene looks desolate, but ash makes fertile soil, and vegetation will quickly return.

Where thicker, viscous lava inches slowly forwards, a black crust forms on top and beneath as it cools. Even when the outside cools and hardens, the inside can stay hot for weeks. Occasionally, a tongue of red-hot, molten rock breaks through the leading edge of the flow.

A dark flow of gassy a'a, thrown out in the earlier eruption, hardens into brittle chunks full of bubbles. It sticks together in crumbly, sharp piles, which are light and crispy at the surface, but thicker and more blocky lower down. Cooled flows of a'a are very rough and difficult to walk over.

a'a A Hawaiian word used to describe a bubbly lava that cools to form a rough, brittle surface.

tephra Fragments of rock and lava of any size that are thrown out during explosive volcanic eruptions.

sulphur Yellow substance deposited as crystals around vents and fumeroles. Sulphur dioxide is a volcanic gas that is harmful to the lungs.

VOLCANIC EJECTA

Anything thrown out of a volcano is called ejecta. There are many different types, which harden into sparkling strings of volcanic glass, spongy stones that float on water, or massive rocks. Some volcanic ejecta, such as blocks of semi-molten rock, are heavy and potentially lethal, but others may be fragile. The forms ejecta take depend on the type and composition of the lava, how many gas bubbles it contains, and how it cools.

Rounded shape

Pele's Tears

If droplets of lava cool quickly in the air, they make small beads of volcanic glass called Pele's Tears. These are usually dark, but can be transparent. They are formed from the relatively liquid lava of Hawaiian volcanoes.

Size	Mainly 2–4 mm ($\frac{1}{10}$–$\frac{1}{6}$ in)
Made of	Obsidian (volcanic glass)
Dispersion	Surrounding region
Uses	Jewellery
Hazards	Low risk

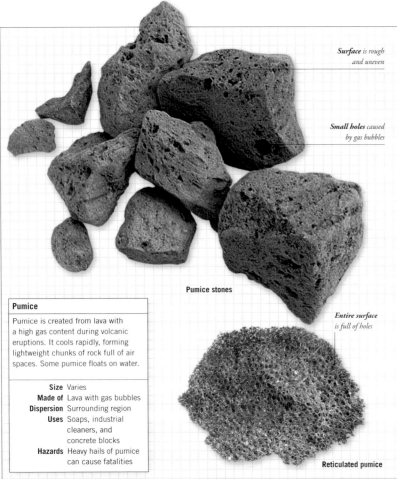

Surface is rough and uneven

Small holes caused by gas bubbles

Pumice stones

Entire surface is full of holes

Reticulated pumice

Pumice

Pumice is created from lava with a high gas content during volcanic eruptions. It cools rapidly, forming lightweight chunks of rock full of air spaces. Some pumice floats on water.

Size	Varies
Made of	Lava with gas bubbles
Dispersion	Surrounding region
Uses	Soaps, industrial cleaners, and concrete blocks
Hazards	Heavy hails of pumice can cause fatalities

Volcanic bombs

The fast-moving lumps of magma hurled from a volcano become rounded in mid-air and harden into lava bombs. These bombs come in different sizes and a variety of shapes. Bread-crust bombs are created when a hard crust forms around a core of hot gases – as the gas escapes, the outer crust cracks. Cowpat bombs are still hot and liquid when they crash into the ground, and splatter on impact. Lava bombs may react with oxygen in the air to develop a reddish colour when they cool. Some also become darker in colour.

Size	From 64 cm (25 in) to several metres	**Uses**	Various in industry, including building
Made of	Lava	**Hazards**	Can cause fatalities and damage buildings
Dispersion	Local area only		

Deep cracks on surface

Bread-crust bomb

Flattened shape caused by impact

Cowpat bomb

Basalt rock

Rocky volcanic bomb

Obsidian

Surface is smooth and shiny

When lava cools too fast for crystals to form, it becomes obsidian, or volcanic glass. Usually it is jet-black or dark greenish black. Many cultures have made jewellery or sacrificial knives from this shiny, razor-sharp rock.

Size	Varies
Made of	Very viscous lava
Dispersion	Surrounding region
Uses	Jewellery, weapons, and decorative items
Hazards	Very sharp when broken

Sharp blade

Obsidian

Obsidian knife

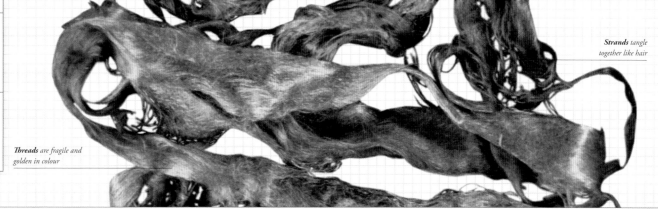

Pele's Hair

These delicate threads of volcanic glass resemble human hair. Named after the Hawaiian goddess of fire, they form when lava fountains hurl strands of molten volcanic glass into the air, and strong winds stretch them.

Size	Up to 2 m (6½ ft) in length
Made of	Obsidian (volcanic glass)
Dispersion	Surrounding region
Uses	None
Hazards	Low risk

Strands tangle together like hair

Threads are fragile and golden in colour

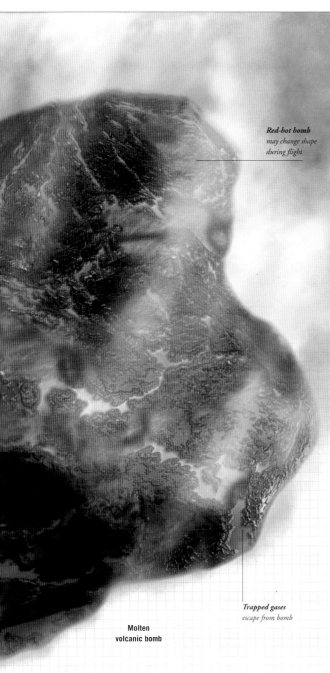

Red-hot bomb may change shape during flight

Trapped gases escape from bomb

Molten volcanic bomb

Ash

Volcanic ash is a fine, grey or whitish powder made from shattered volcanic rock and glass particles. It is very light, and may be carried a long way – even round the world – before falling.

Size	Particles up to 2 mm (1/10 in) across
Made of	Tiny fragments of rock and glass
Dispersion	Often vast areas
Uses	Various in industry
Hazards	Danger to aircraft; breathing problems

Ash builds up to form thick layer

Lava flow solidifies as it cools down

Jumble of rough, irregularly shaped rocks

Lava flow

When lava flows from a volcano, it hardens in streams or piles, depending on how thick it is and how fast it flows. Lava in contact with the ground and air hardens first, but the crust is constantly broken by hot lava rolling inside it.

Size	Varies
Made of	Molten rock
Dispersion	Local area only
Uses	Construction materials and road-building
Hazards	Large flows may bury people and buildings

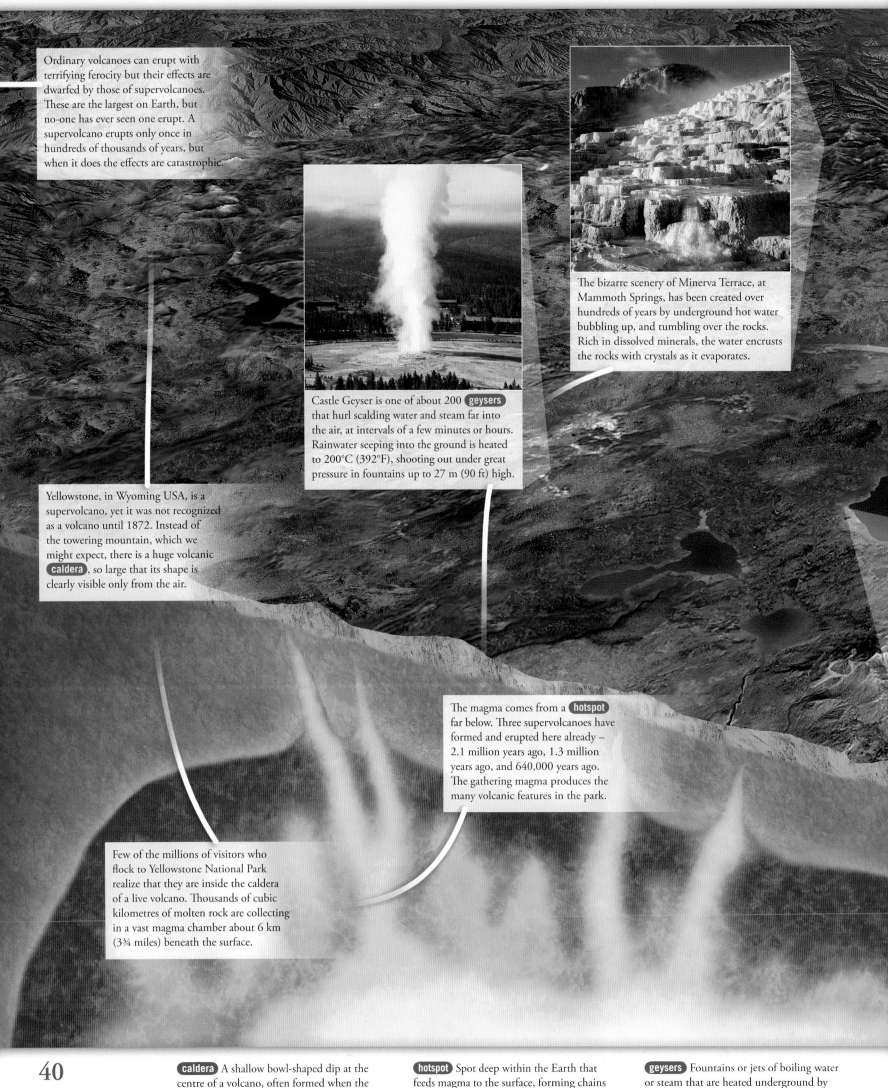

Ordinary volcanoes can erupt with terrifying ferocity but their effects are dwarfed by those of supervolcanoes. These are the largest on Earth, but no-one has ever seen one erupt. A supervolcano erupts only once in hundreds of thousands of years, but when it does the effects are catastrophic.

The bizarre scenery of Minerva Terrace, at Mammoth Springs, has been created over hundreds of years by underground hot water bubbling up, and tumbling over the rocks. Rich in dissolved minerals, the water encrusts the rocks with crystals as it evaporates.

Castle Geyser is one of about 200 **geysers** that hurl scalding water and steam far into the air, at intervals of a few minutes or hours. Rainwater seeping into the ground is heated to 200°C (392°F), shooting out under great pressure in fountains up to 27 m (90 ft) high.

Yellowstone, in Wyoming USA, is a supervolcano, yet it was not recognized as a volcano until 1872. Instead of the towering mountain, which we might expect, there is a huge volcanic **caldera**, so large that its shape is clearly visible only from the air.

The magma comes from a **hotspot** far below. Three supervolcanoes have formed and erupted here already – 2.1 million years ago, 1.3 million years ago, and 640,000 years ago. The gathering magma produces the many volcanic features in the park.

Few of the millions of visitors who flock to Yellowstone National Park realize that they are inside the caldera of a live volcano. Thousands of cubic kilometres of molten rock are collecting in a vast magma chamber about 6 km (3¾ miles) beneath the surface.

caldera A shallow bowl-shaped dip at the centre of a volcano, often formed when the magma chamber collapses after an eruption.

hotspot Spot deep within the Earth that feeds magma to the surface, forming chains of hotspot volcanoes, such as Hawaii.

geysers Fountains or jets of boiling water or steam that are heated underground by hot volcanic rock and spout at intervals.

SUPERVOLCANO

Satellites in space keep a watchful eye on the caldera at Yellowstone, taking pictures and measuring movement in the ground. The massive caldera could explode in the next 50,000 years in an eruption over 500 times greater than the one that destroyed Pompeii. It would scatter ash over the United States and change the world's climate. Yellowstone is also monitored for the smaller-scale eruptions that are more likely to happen.

Yellowstone's own Grand Canyon is a winding **ravine**, which plunges 365 m (1,200 ft) at its deepest. It was gouged from the rock, between 10,000 and 14,000 years ago, by torrents of water released as massive ice dams melted after the last ice age.

Yellowstone Lake hides the giant caldera produced by the last eruption at Yellowstone, when the ground collapsed into the magma chamber. In the north, the bed of the lake bulges upwards as the magma chamber beneath continues to swell.

In Fountain Paint Pot, thick domes of mud swell and burst in the **mudpot**, spurting hot volcanic gases, mud, and steam into the air. Some solidify into short-lived mud volcanoes that can grow to 4 m (13 ft) tall. They collapse in winter when the mud becomes watery.

ravine A deep, narrow opening between hills.

mudpot An area of sticky, bubbling mud, formed by hot water from underground forcing its way up through soil rich in volcanic ash.

VOLCANIC LANDSCAPES

Volcanoes have left their mark on the landscape in many ways. As well as mountains, they have created islands, lakes, and rock formations. This volcanic panorama might appear to belong to the world of science fiction, but it reveals many weird and wonderful features that exist on the Earth today.

In ancient eruptions, millions of years ago, massive floods of liquid **basalt** poured from countless **fissures** to cover vast areas of land in a layer several kilometres thick. Over thousands of years, wind and water have carved strange rocky towers from these deep flows of basalt rock.

New islands can also rise dramatically from the sea. Surtur's Island (Surtsey), near Iceland, emerged in 1963. It was created by lava from a fissure piling up on the sea floor. As more and more lava erupted, the mound grew large enough to appear above the water.

Whole islands can be destroyed by the powerful mix of volcanic activity and water. The Greek island of Santorini, or Thera, in the Aegean Sea, was once a huge volcano. In about 1410 BC, the island blew apart, leaving only a remnant in the shape of a horseshoe.

Hot, molten rock still pours from fissures in the ground in Iceland. It is the only place on Earth where the spreading that takes place at mid-ocean ridges can be seen on land. The heat under the ground also drives up geysers that spurt scalding steam.

Where the crust is thin, and magma is close to the surface, **geothermal** power stations are built to take heat from the ground and convert it into electricity. Steam and super-heated water are drawn up to drive turbines, which then power generators.

basalt A fine-grained, dark volcanic rock formed from cooled lava. Most of the rock that forms the oceanic crust is basalt.

fissures Long cracks in the ground. They are often opened up by landslips or earthquakes.

geothermal Using the Earth's internal heat. Geothermal energy is extracted from the ground in areas of volcanic activity.

The mixture of sea water and magma produces an explosion driven by steam. The magma cools rapidly as it meets the freezing water, and is thrown out in a shower of fragments. Surtur's Island grew by erupting in this way, between 1963 and 1967.

A **cinder cone** can grow quickly in a single, long burst of volcanic activity. The classic cone shape builds up from ash and tephra piling up around the bowl-shaped vent, often on the sides or base of a much larger volcano. Cinder cones often occur in clusters.

Stratovolcanoes produce violent **Strombolian eruptions**. They can hurl vast lava bombs into the sky and throw out spectacular showers of fiery ash in great fountains. Falling debris blankets the slopes, adding to the mountain's size with each eruption.

A **stratovolcano** builds in the same way as a cinder cone, but over hundreds, or even hundreds of thousands, of years. Within just weeks of an eruption, deep channels appear in its flanks as loose, soft material washes away.

A crater lake can form when a volcano finally erodes away, or collapses after a cataclysmic eruption, and the crater fills with water. The lake may be a startling colour because the water often contains chemicals, which are sometimes highly toxic.

cinder cone A small, steep-sided volcano with a central crater, formed from solidified lava fragments. Also called a scoria cone.

stratovolcano A volcano with steep sides, built from layers of ash and lava.

Strombolian eruptions These erupt from a vent or crater, with a series of short-lived explosions sending sticky basalt lava into the air.

The eruptions that form shield volcanoes burst from fissures and rifts rather than central craters. They spit long curtains of fiery lava far into the air, sometimes for years at a time. The lava pours down the slopes, cascading over rocks like a burning waterfall.

A shield volcano also builds up gradually from lava oozing out of the ground, often growing from the sea bed into islands. The shield volcanoes of Hawaii are the biggest volcanoes on Earth, formed by lava piling up over hundreds of thousands of years.

Other shapes grow from within. A lava dome is a squat pile of lava that has been squeezed out of the ground, often on the flank or inside the crater of a volcano. The lava is too viscous to run downhill. It moves only sluggishly if at all, and piles up over the vent.

In Cappadocia, Turkey, erosion by wind, rain, and sand has carved unearthly shapes from compacted layers of volcanic ash. These eerie reminders of long-dead volcanoes are made of a soft rock called **tuff**, which is easily worn away.

tuff A soft rock, formed when layers of ash mix with water and are compressed.

Plinian eruption A large, explosive eruption producing huge, dark columns of ash and tephra, rising high into the air.

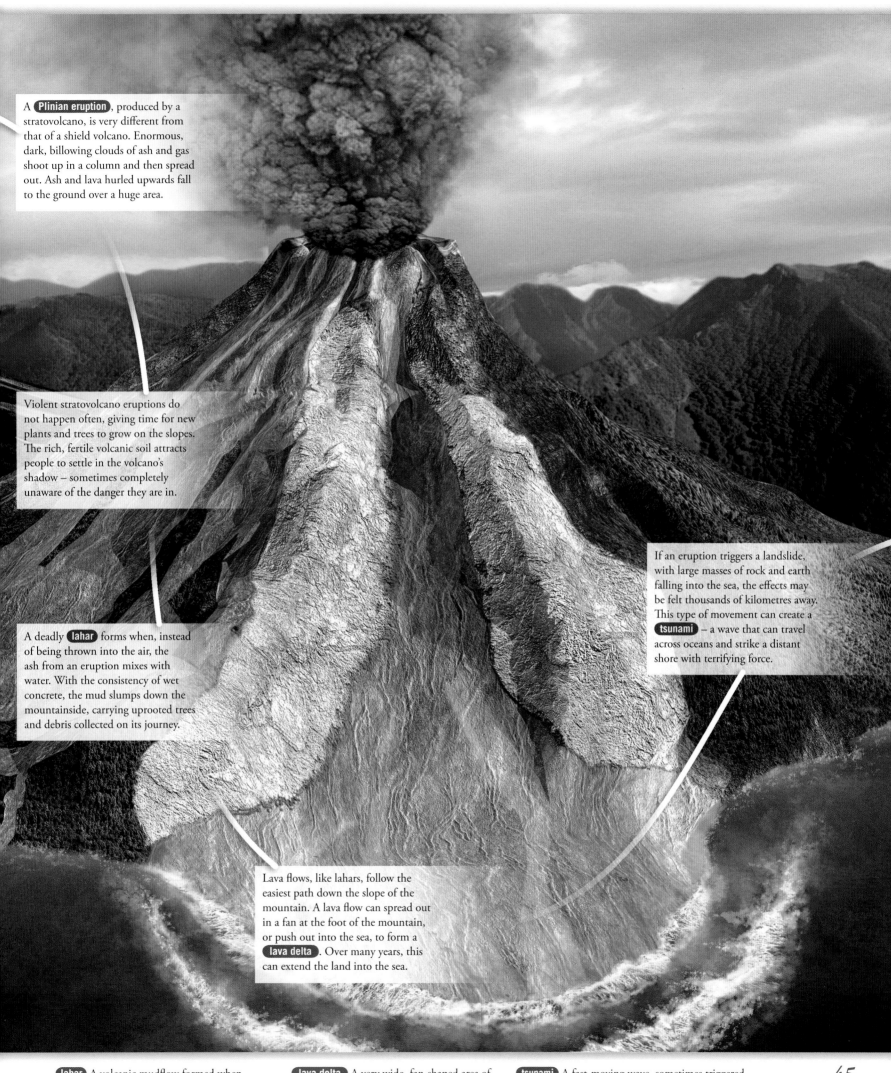

A **Plinian eruption**, produced by a stratovolcano, is very different from that of a shield volcano. Enormous, dark, billowing clouds of ash and gas shoot up in a column and then spread out. Ash and lava hurled upwards fall to the ground over a huge area.

Violent stratovolcano eruptions do not happen often, giving time for new plants and trees to grow on the slopes. The rich, fertile volcanic soil attracts people to settle in the volcano's shadow – sometimes completely unaware of the danger they are in.

A deadly **lahar** forms when, instead of being thrown into the air, the ash from an eruption mixes with water. With the consistency of wet concrete, the mud slumps down the mountainside, carrying uprooted trees and debris collected on its journey.

If an eruption triggers a landslide, with large masses of rock and earth falling into the sea, the effects may be felt thousands of kilometres away. This type of movement can create a **tsunami** – a wave that can travel across oceans and strike a distant shore with terrifying force.

Lava flows, like lahars, follow the easiest path down the slope of the mountain. A lava flow can spread out in a fan at the foot of the mountain, or push out into the sea, to form a **lava delta**. Over many years, this can extend the land into the sea.

lahar A volcanic mudflow formed when water from heavy rain, rivers, or melted snow, mixes with ash.

lava delta A very wide, fan-shaped area of land that is formed when lava meets the sea.

tsunami A fast-moving wave, sometimes triggered by an earthquake or volcanic eruption, which rapidly gains height as it reaches shallow water.

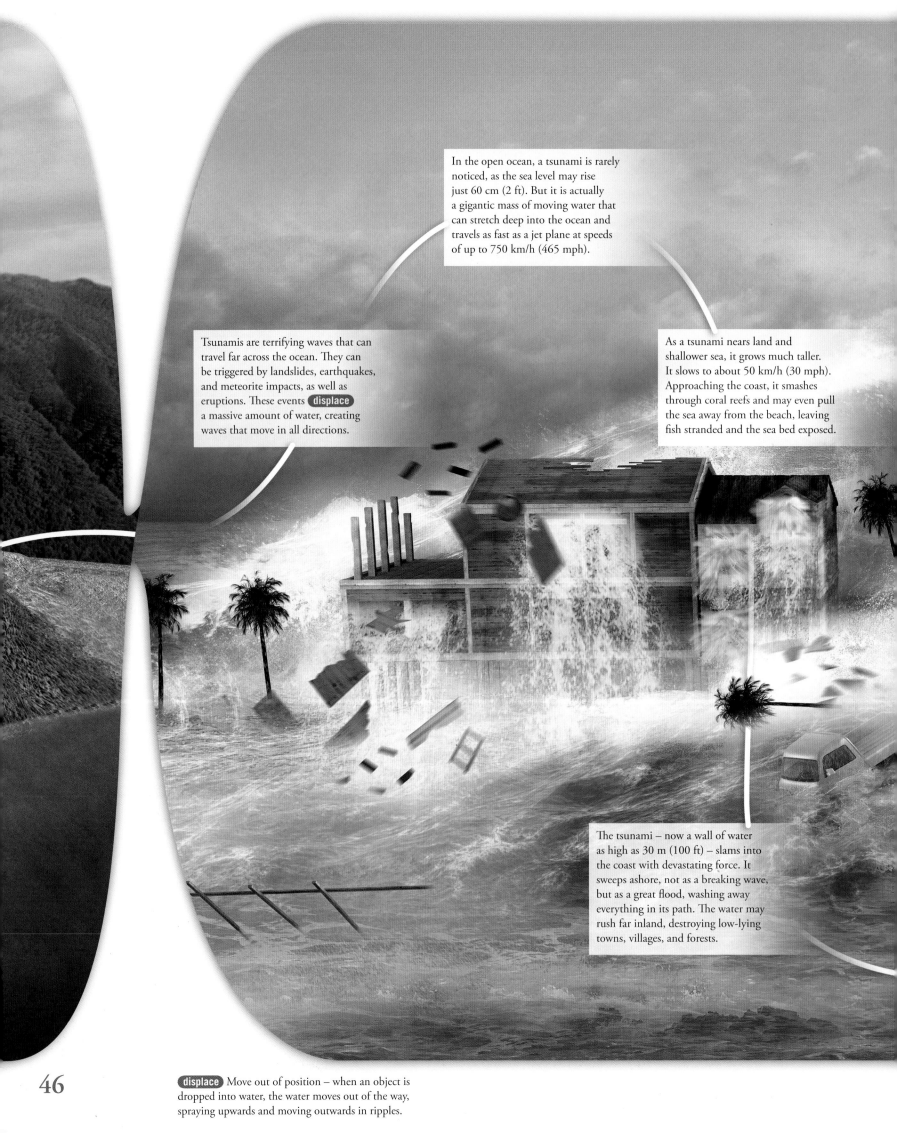

In the open ocean, a tsunami is rarely noticed, as the sea level may rise just 60 cm (2 ft). But it is actually a gigantic mass of moving water that can stretch deep into the ocean and travels as fast as a jet plane at speeds of up to 750 km/h (465 mph).

Tsunamis are terrifying waves that can travel far across the ocean. They can be triggered by landslides, earthquakes, and meteorite impacts, as well as eruptions. These events **displace** a massive amount of water, creating waves that move in all directions.

As a tsunami nears land and shallower sea, it grows much taller. It slows to about 50 km/h (30 mph). Approaching the coast, it smashes through coral reefs and may even pull the sea away from the beach, leaving fish stranded and the sea bed exposed.

The tsunami – now a wall of water as high as 30 m (100 ft) – slams into the coast with devastating force. It sweeps ashore, not as a breaking wave, but as a great flood, washing away everything in its path. The water may rush far inland, destroying low-lying towns, villages, and forests.

displace Move out of position – when an object is dropped into water, the water moves out of the way, spraying upwards and moving outwards in ripples.

TSUNAMI 2004

In December 2004, a catastrophic tsunami killed at least 200,000 people. It was caused by a massive undersea earthquake off the coast of Indonesia, which lasted 10 minutes and made the whole planet shake. The waves that followed travelled right around the world, wreaking havoc along the coastlines of Indonesia, Thailand, Sri Lanka, India, and Africa. This tsunami was the worst on record and one of the most extensive natural disasters in human history.

Gleebruk, Indonesia, April 2004

Gleebruk, Indonesia, January 2005

The first wave is rarely the last. Tsunamis are multiple waves, and can be up to 700 km (430 miles) apart. There may be a gap of minutes or even an hour, then a second wave sweeps in, horrifying those who thought the danger had passed.

A tsunami may come as a terrible shock to people living near the coast. The waves can race across the ocean in a few hours, crashing into areas that felt no other effects from the earthquake or volcano that triggered the disaster.

As it pours inland, the tsunami brings with it a terrible tide of debris – smashed buildings, cars, boats, uprooted trees, and even people and animals. When it finally recedes, it can carry its victims and wreckage out to sea with it.

KRAKATAU
THE EXPLOSION THAT ROCKED THE WORLD

Krakatau lies between Indonesia's two largest islands, Sumatra and Java, and in the middle of the Sunda Straits, an important and busy shipping route.

During the summer of 1883, people living near the tiny Asian island of Krakatau became used to seeing clouds of smoke and steam rise high into the air. They heard the mountain rumbling and cracking, and visitors to the uninhabited island found it covered in a deep layer of ash. But they were not prepared for the island to explode, blowing itself away in a massive eruption on 27 August.

The island's last days

Krakatau sprang into life after 200 years of peace by shooting a dense column of ash and steam into the sky in May 1883. Over the coming weeks, more explosions and ash falls entertained spectators – some even took boat trips to watch the volcano's noisy displays.

"Chains of fire appeared to ascend and descend between the volcano and the sky."

Captain W. J. Watson, of the cargo ship Charles Bal, *which was sailing from Northern Ireland to Hong Kong*

"We saw a gigantic wave of prodigious height advancing toward the shore."

Eyewitness on the ship Loudon, *in Lampong Bay, Sumatra, where waves tore boats from their moorings*

This engraving of Krakatau appeared in Harper's Weekly, *an American news and literary journal, in August 1883.*

On 11 August, a government surveyor visited the volcano. He was the last person to set foot on the island. The official found it cloaked in toxic fumes, the forests burned, and the land covered in a layer of ash. Far worse was to come.

Krakatau rages

Just after noon on 26 August, an explosion shook the mountain. It sent a column of black smoke far into the sky. By the next day, the column stretched up 50 km (31 miles) – five times

KRAKATAU TIMELINE

20 May 1883 Krakatau bursts into life.
6.00 am Ash and steam shoot up 11,000 m (36,000 ft).
10.55 am Tremors are felt in the Javan town of Batavia (now called Jakarta), 133 km (83 miles) to the east.

June Dutch engineer A. Schuurman visits Krakatau, taking geological samples and climbing to the crater.
Mid-June Ships in the Sunda Straits, between Sumatra and Java, report pumice in the water and heavy ash falls.

26 August, 12.53 pm First blast from Krakatau sends out black clouds, debris, and powerful shockwaves.
Afternoon and evening The vibrations and explosions rapidly grow in strength, and the sea becomes violent.

as high as a jumbo jet flies. At some point, one of the explosions tore the island apart. The shockwaves triggered the deadly tsunamis – 18 in all – that swept through the region.

Day becomes night
No-one knows what it was like on the island of Krakatau during the eruption, but on Java, to the east, local people heard one explosion after another.

Rising out of Krakatau's caldera, Anak Krakatau is still growing and erupts frequently.

The temperature dropped from 27°C to 18°C (81°F to 64°F), it grew dark in the middle of the day, and all sounds were muffled by the huge amount of ash in the air. On Sumatra, to the west, it was much more serious. During the evening of 26 August, the sea withdrew and then crashed back into the shore as a tsunami struck. On some nearby islands, the wave wrecked everything.

Land on fire
Some of the residents of Sumatra managed to escape to high ground, but they were pummelled by a hail of falling pumice, choked by scalding ash, and lashed by searing, hurricane-force winds. Fiery blasts raged across the land, setting fire to the

jungle and houses. One of the few survivors was Mrs Beyerinck, who lived in Ketimbang, about 40 km (24 miles) north of Krakatau. She reported that, "It became pitch dark. The last thing I saw was the ash being pushed up through the cracks in the floorboards, like a fountain… It seemed as if the air was being sucked away and I could not breathe." Daylight did not return until the afternoon of 29 August, but as the darkness lifted, it revealed a hellish scene of destruction.

Lasting impact
About 36,500 people died, most of whom were killed by the tsunamis. For weeks, both sea and land were covered with tangled trees, fallen buildings, dead bodies, and chunks of coral ripped from the sea bed. Ash carried high into the atmosphere produced brilliantly coloured sunsets for the next three years, as far away as London and New York. It also blocked the heat from the Sun, so that temperatures dropped and weather was disrupted all over the world for five years.

The island regrows
Interest in Krakatau was immense – scientists studied its geology, watched the reappearance of plants and animals on the island, and logged the weather changes with great care. It was the first volcanic eruption to be fully investigated. Scientists around the world explored how and why such a catastrophe could happen. From Krakatau's ruins a new volcano has been born. Anak Krakatau, meaning "Child of Krakatau", started to rise in 1927. Its growth has been watched and recorded in minute detail. One day it, too, will tear itself apart.

> "So violent are the explosions that the ear-drums of over half my crew have been shattered…"
>
> *Captain Sampson, of the British vessel* Norham Castle, *writing notes in his official log*

Volcanic ash

Pumice stone

Thick clouds of ash and pumice stones from the eruption showered across a wide area and blotted out sunlight for two days. Ten months later, rafts of floating pumice in the Indian Ocean were still thick enough to walk on.

Devastating facts
Once, Krakatau was a densely forested and beautiful island. But over two days in 1883 it was virtually blasted out of existence by a series of Plinian eruptions – including the biggest explosion in modern times.

Explosion	The blast from the largest explosion on the morning of 27 August was probably the loudest noise in recorded history.
Waves of sound	Sound waves from the eruptions went around the globe at least three times.
Weird effects	So much ash and gas entered the Earth's atmosphere during the eruptions that the Sun and Moon appeared first blue, then green.
Blown apart	Two-thirds of the island of Krakatau was totally destroyed by the blasts. All three volcanic peaks on the island, including Krakatau itself, toppled.
Sea bed crater	Krakatau's massively enlarged caldera left a gaping hole in the ocean floor, and flooded with sea water to a depth of 300 m (985 ft).
Tsunamis	Eighteen waves raced across the sea from the collapsing island, gathering height as they neared land. The largest reached 30 m (100 ft) tall.
Terrible force	The tsunamis wreaked havoc along the region's coastlines, and swept the debris of boats and villages far inland. A 2-m (6½-ft) wave reached Auckland in New Zealand, having travelled a total of 7,767 km (4,823) miles.
Death toll	About 4,500 people fell victim to falling ash or pumice or to red-hot *nuées ardentes* (glowing clouds). The vast majority of the casualties – 32,000 people – were killed by the tsunamis.

Anak Krakatau erupts fountains of red-hot ash and hurls lava bombs, but it lacks the power of its parent.

8.00 pm Tsunamis devastate several coastal towns.
27 August, 5.30 am A series of five gigantic explosions begins, releasing deadly ash clouds and hails of pumice, and triggering yet more tsunamis.

10.02 am The fourth, and largest, explosion tears Krakatau to pieces.
29 August Daylight breaks through for the first time in two days.

RECORD BREAKERS

There are record-breaking volcanoes all around the world, and even on other planets. Volcanoes take many forms. They may live briefly, growing and dying in just a few years. Others take a slower pace, rising from the ground over thousands of years and lying quiet for centuries between eruptions. Some put on stunning displays of fireworks that draw tourists, but they may also devastate huge areas with cataclysmic eruptions.

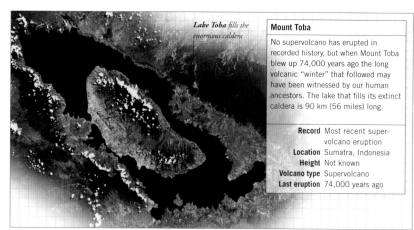

Lake Toba fills the enormous caldera

Mount Toba

No supervolcano has erupted in recorded history, but when Mount Toba blew up 74,000 years ago the long volcanic "winter" that followed may have been witnessed by our human ancestors. The lake that fills its extinct caldera is 90 km (56 miles) long.

Record	Most recent super-volcano eruption
Location	Sumatra, Indonesia
Height	Not known
Volcano type	Supervolcano
Last eruption	74,000 years ago

Upper slopes are a barren wasteland of ash and old lava

Large ash cone near to summit

Main crater

Mount Etna

Near-neighbours Mount Etna and Stromboli are extremely active volcanoes. Etna is about 2.5 million years old. It has four active craters, with about 200 ash cones on its sides, and erupts every few years.

Record	Oldest eruptive volcano
Location	Sicily, Italy
Height	3.3 km (2 miles)
Volcano type	Stratovolcano on top of a shield volcano
Last eruption	2002

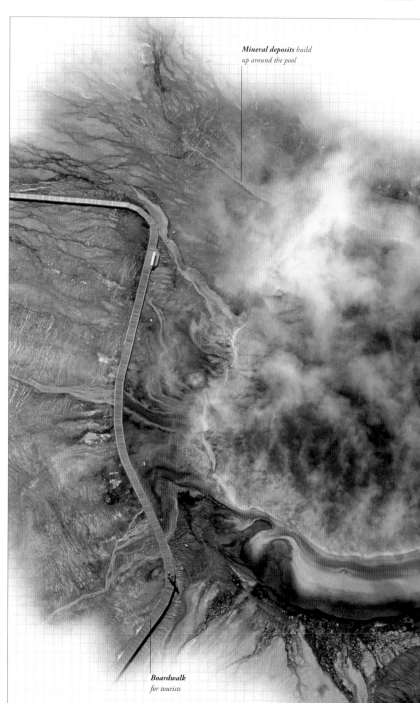

Mineral deposits build up around the pool

Boardwalk for tourists

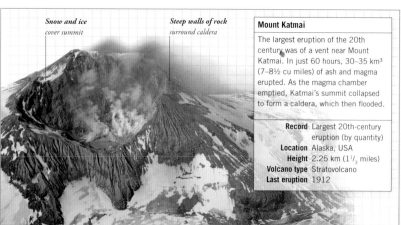

Snow and ice cover summit

Steep walls of rock surround caldera

Mount Katmai

The largest eruption of the 20th century was of a vent near Mount Katmai. In just 60 hours, 30–35 km³ (7–8½ cu miles) of ash and magma erupted. As the magma chamber emptied, Katmai's summit collapsed to form a caldera, which then flooded.

Record	Largest 20th-century eruption (by quantity)
Location	Alaska, USA
Height	2.25 km (1¹/₂ miles)
Volcano type	Stratovolcano
Last eruption	1912

Church half-buried by lava

Paricutín

Paricutín gave scientists a unique chance to watch a volcano from birth. It began to grow in a field in Mexico in 1943, rising 336 m (1,100 ft) in the first year. It erupted continuously until 1952 and then fell silent.

Record	Fastest-growing volcano on record
Location	Mexico
Height	900 m (2,950 ft)
Volcano type	Scoria cone
Last eruption	1943–1952

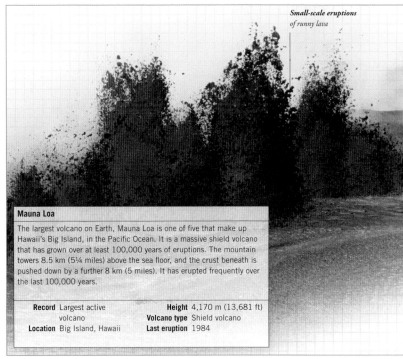

Small-scale eruptions of runny lava

Mauna Loa

The largest volcano on Earth, Mauna Loa is one of five that make up Hawaii's Big Island, in the Pacific Ocean. It is a massive shield volcano that has grown over at least 100,000 years of eruptions. The mountain towers 8.5 km (5¼ miles) above the sea floor, and the crust beneath is pushed down by a further 8 km (5 miles). It has erupted frequently over the last 100,000 years.

Record	Largest active volcano	**Height**	4,170 m (13,681 ft)
Location	Big Island, Hawaii	**Volcano type**	Shield volcano
		Last eruption	1984

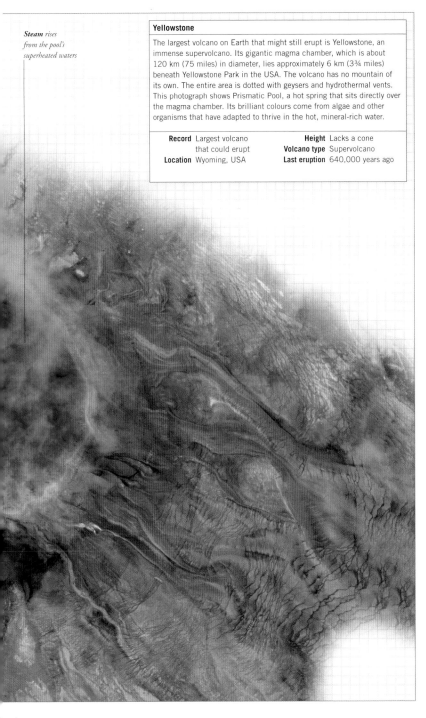

Steam rises from the pool's superheated waters

Yellowstone

The largest volcano on Earth that might still erupt is Yellowstone, an immense supervolcano. Its gigantic magma chamber, which is about 120 km (75 miles) in diameter, lies approximately 6 km (3¾ miles) beneath Yellowstone Park in the USA. The volcano has no mountain of its own. The entire area is dotted with geysers and hydrothermal vents. This photograph shows Prismatic Pool, a hot spring that sits directly over the magma chamber. Its brilliant colours come from algae and other organisms that have adapted to thrive in the hot, mineral-rich water.

Record	Largest volcano that could erupt	**Height**	Lacks a cone
		Volcano type	Supervolcano
Location	Wyoming, USA	**Last eruption**	640,000 years ago

Lower slopes of volcano are fertile farmland

Vesuvius

Vesuvius towers over the city of Naples, Italy. Three million people live in its shadow – more than any other active volcano in Europe. Naples has an evacuation plan to move everyone to safety at one week's notice.

Record	Most populated European volcano
Location	Campania, Italy
Height	1,281 m (4,203 ft)
Volcano type	Stratovolcano
Last eruption	1944

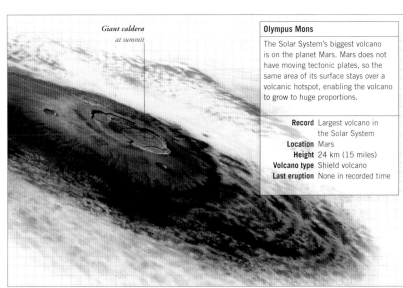

Giant caldera at summit

Olympus Mons

The Solar System's biggest volcano is on the planet Mars. Mars does not have moving tectonic plates, so the same area of its surface stays over a volcanic hotspot, enabling the volcano to grow to huge proportions.

Record	Largest volcano in the Solar System
Location	Mars
Height	24 km (15 miles)
Volcano type	Shield volcano
Last eruption	None in recorded time

PYROCLASTIC BLAST

Record-breaking eruptions often begin with one or more immense explosions that rip apart a volcanic mountain with more force than an atomic bomb. The impact of the blast is earth shattering, hurling scalding gases, ash, molten lava, and massive chunks of rock far into the sky. This type of explosive eruption is the most dangerous. Flying debris from the volcano can travel several kilometres, falling to earth with terrible, deadly force.

Pressure may have been building inside the volcano for centuries, as magma gathers inside it. Eventually, the mountain can take no more and gives way. The first blast cracks it open, splitting the rock. The pressure inside the dome plummets – an eruption is about to begin.

The second explosion shatters more of the volcano. Another torrent of rock and ash streams out. Again, the gaping hole reduces the pressure and more magma explodes within. Bang after bang tears the volcano apart, sometimes over a period of months.

Gigantic chunks of rock, torn from the site of the explosion, tumble in a cascading landslide down the side of the volcano. Steam, gases, and ash stream out of the newly opened crater, but there is little or no molten lava to be seen.

Inside the volcano, the drop in pressure bursts all the bubbles in the magma, shattering it into ash. This causes the magma to expand immensely, and the surrounding rock can hold it no longer. The magma explodes with an enormous bang.

pyroclastic explosion An explosion of fragments of volcanic rock during a violent eruption.

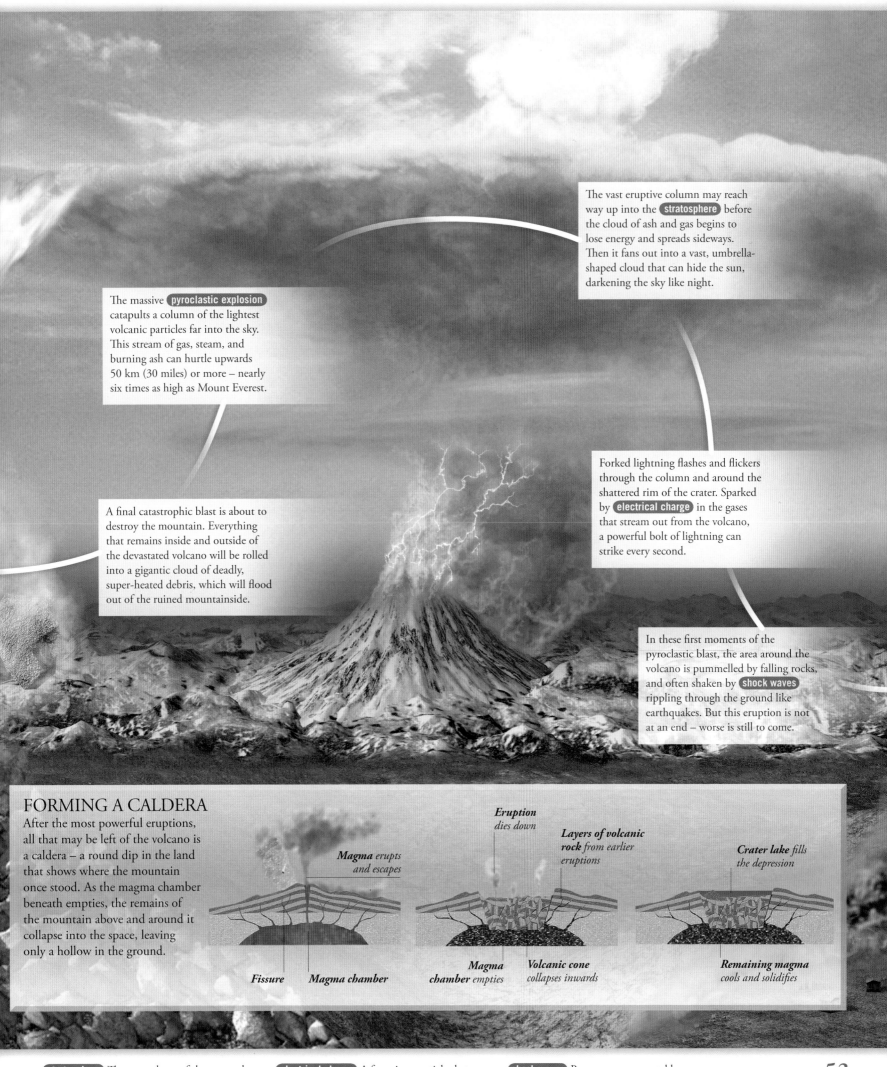

The vast eruptive column may reach way up into the **stratosphere** before the cloud of ash and gas begins to lose energy and spreads sideways. Then it fans out into a vast, umbrella-shaped cloud that can hide the sun, darkening the sky like night.

The massive **pyroclastic explosion** catapults a column of the lightest volcanic particles far into the sky. This stream of gas, steam, and burning ash can hurtle upwards 50 km (30 miles) or more – nearly six times as high as Mount Everest.

Forked lightning flashes and flickers through the column and around the shattered rim of the crater. Sparked by **electrical charge** in the gases that stream out from the volcano, a powerful bolt of lightning can strike every second.

A final catastrophic blast is about to destroy the mountain. Everything that remains inside and outside of the devastated volcano will be rolled into a gigantic cloud of deadly, super-heated debris, which will flood out of the ruined mountainside.

In these first moments of the pyroclastic blast, the area around the volcano is pummelled by falling rocks, and often shaken by **shock waves** rippling through the ground like earthquakes. But this eruption is not at an end – worse is still to come.

FORMING A CALDERA

After the most powerful eruptions, all that may be left of the volcano is a caldera – a round dip in the land that shows where the mountain once stood. As the magma chamber beneath empties, the remains of the mountain above and around it collapse into the space, leaving only a hollow in the ground.

Magma erupts and escapes

Fissure *Magma chamber*

Eruption dies down

Layers of volcanic rock from earlier eruptions

Magma chamber empties *Volcanic cone collapses inwards*

Crater lake fills the depression

Remaining magma cools and solidifies

stratosphere The upper layer of the atmosphere, between about 8–16 km (5–10 miles) to 50 km (30 miles) above the Earth.

electrical charge A force in a particle that attracts or repels other particles, producing static electricity.

shock waves Pressure waves caused by an explosion or an earthquake. They vibrate through the Earth, causing movement.

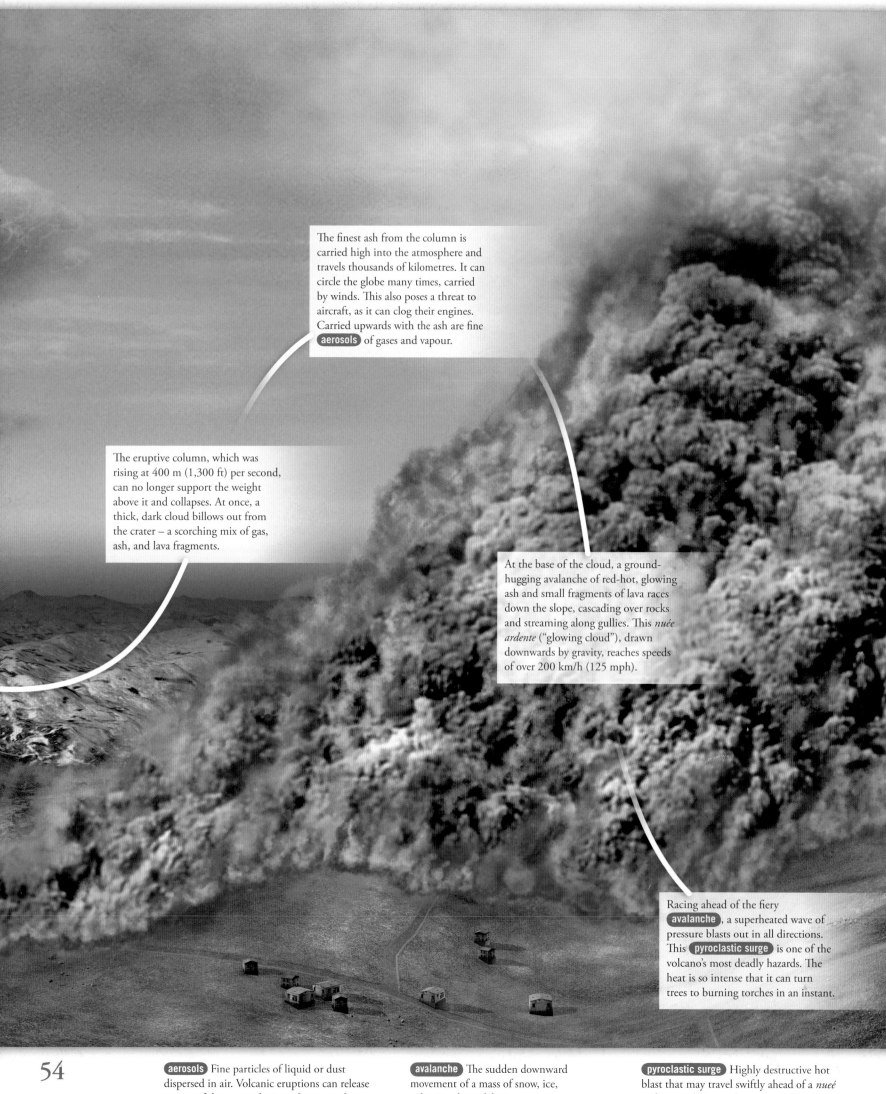

The finest ash from the column is carried high into the atmosphere and travels thousands of kilometres. It can circle the globe many times, carried by winds. This also poses a threat to aircraft, as it can clog their engines. Carried upwards with the ash are fine **aerosols** of gases and vapour.

The eruptive column, which was rising at 400 m (1,300 ft) per second, can no longer support the weight above it and collapses. At once, a thick, dark cloud billows out from the crater – a scorching mix of gas, ash, and lava fragments.

At the base of the cloud, a ground-hugging avalanche of red-hot, glowing ash and small fragments of lava races down the slope, cascading over rocks and streaming along gullies. This *nuée ardente* ("glowing cloud"), drawn downwards by gravity, reaches speeds of over 200 km/h (125 mph).

Racing ahead of the fiery **avalanche**, a superheated wave of pressure blasts out in all directions. This **pyroclastic surge** is one of the volcano's most deadly hazards. The heat is so intense that it can turn trees to burning torches in an instant.

aerosols Fine particles of liquid or dust dispersed in air. Volcanic eruptions can release tonnes of these particles into the atmosphere.

avalanche The sudden downward movement of a mass of snow, ice, volcanic ash, or debris.

pyroclastic surge Highly destructive hot blast that may travel swiftly ahead of a *nueé ardente*, and over wider areas.

No-one overtaken by the cloud would be able to see or breathe. Just a few breaths of searing hot gas and volcanic ash would be deadly. This **electron micrograph** of an ash deposit reveals the tiny, choking particles of rock that can clog the lungs.

Often the first pyroclastic surge is followed by others, sometimes hours or even days later. If more of the dome collapses, another surge may blast down the slope, perhaps in a different direction, destroying anything that escaped the first time.

As the gas it contains finally cools, the billowing cloud drops down, carrying its cargo of light ash to earth. The ash may settle in a layer many metres thick near to the volcano, but a fine ash fall may be found hundreds of kilometres away from the eruption.

Incinerating everything in its path, the flow rips silently through the landscape at 300 km/h (185 mph), at temperatures of up to 800°C (1,470°F). The surge may stretch for 100 km (60 miles) before its energy ebbs away. Running ahead of it to escape would be useless.

electron micrograph Image taken of an object with a very powerful microscope called an electron microscope.

The newly laid layers of ash and thick, volcanic mud that blanket the slopes of the volcano will eventually harden. While the layers are still soft, water running down the mountainside quickly cuts **gullies** in the new surface, giving it a ridged appearance.

The crater is now cold and exposed, revealing a new, shattered profile. Rock has been blasted away from the rim, and the whole of the **summit** may have been blown away. But the volcano lives on. Within a few weeks, a new **lava dome** is swelling in the bottom of the wrecked crater.

Outside the area devastated by the flow of ash, mud, and lava, wildlife has not escaped unharmed. Poisonous gases in the air and chemicals or ash in the water can kill plants and animals living around the mountain. These damaging effects may last for many months.

The volcano's destructive energy is finally spent for now. The area all around is completely devastated, devoid of life, and stripped to bare rock. All looks calm, but the ground may be shaken violently for a year or more by **aftershocks** and further pyroclastic surges.

aftershocks Less powerful tremors following an earthquake or volcanic eruption.

gullies Deep gorges worn into a slope by flowing water.

summit The highest point in a volcano or mountain.

SUNSCREEN

A thick layer of fine ash coated trees, trucks, and buildings in the wake of the 1991 eruption of Mount Pinatubo in the Philippines. A massive eruption like this one can spray a huge volume of tiny particles far into the sky, blocking out the sunlight. As well as ash, the column may include a fine stream of chemical droplets and gases, called aerosols. The orange area on this satellite image is a band of aerosols circling the Earth. Taken two months after Mount Pinatubo's eruption, it showed that the aerosols had become more concentrated. Satellite data also revealed that, over the Antarctic, aerosols had caused a loss of ozone. This layer of ozone in the atmosphere protects us from the Sun's harmful ultraviolet radiation.

SATELLITE IMAGE

Vast areas have been swamped by mudflows and ash fall. Some of the ash has been carried hundreds of kilometres. On the mountainside that bore the brunt of the eruption, nothing has survived. Great forests may be torn down, or at least stripped of their leaves and branches.

Lakes and rivers are poisoned with chemicals, and clogged with ash, mud, and fallen trees. The floor of the lake is covered with many metres of volcanic debris dragged from the slopes. On the surface float tangled rafts of tree trunks, other vegetation, and lumps of floating **pumice**.

Everything looks dead – yet within a year, life will begin to return. Insects and small mammals, hidden underground, will surface. Seeds that were buried or have blown in will **germinate**. New birds and larger mammals will venture in. Meanwhile, magma rises again underground…

lava dome A large mound formed by very thick lava that piles up around a vent.

pumice Light volcanic rock, filled with holes left by gas bubbles, formed by frothy magma as it explodes from the crater.

germinate Begin to grow, by sprouting roots and putting out shoots.

MOUNT ST. HELENS
THE MOUNTAIN THAT BLEW APART

North America

Canada

• Seattle

Mount St. Helens

• Portland

USA

At 8:32 am on 17 May 1980, the first blast throws out a plume of ash, gas, and chunks of rock.

Ten seconds later, as more of the unstable north side of the mountain slides away, a massive eruption starts.

Fifteen seconds after that, the bulging mountainside explodes. The pyroclastic flow that followed reached speeds of up to 1,000 km/h (620 mph).

It took just 30 seconds for Mount St. Helens to tear itself apart in its largest eruption for 4,000 years. In the space of two minutes, a huge pyroclastic surge devastated immense tracts of the surrounding land in Washington State, northwest USA, and killed 57 people.

Tales of long ago
Since pioneers and settlers arrived in the Cascade Mountains region, Mount St. Helens had been fairly quiet, with only minor eruptions. But Native Americans in the area had legends about a more violent past when the "fire mountain" hurled out rocks, shaking the Earth and darkening the Sun. By 1980, volcanologists had been watching Mount St. Helens for years. They knew that the next major eruption was due and predicted it would occur before the end of the 20th century.

First rumblings
In March 1980, earthquakes began to rock the volcano. On 27 March, a small explosive eruption threw black ash 3 km (2 miles) into the air. A swelling on the northern flank

of the mountain was a sure sign that magma was collecting underground. Nearby residents were evacuated and minor eruptions continued, attracting geologists and tourists to the mountain. At the end of April, the volcano went quiet again, but the bulge was still growing by over 1 m (3⅓ ft) a day. By 7 May, it was already 2.5 km (1½ miles) wide. Small eruptions restarted, but local people were fed up and wanted to go home.

Sudden catastrophe
With no further warning, on the morning of 18 May, an earthquake shook rocks from the top of the northern side of

> "I have a gut feeling... that, as the bulge continues to grow, something dramatic is going to happen soon."
>
> *Jack Hyde, geologist at Tacoma Community College, 5 May*

MOUNT ST. HELENS TIMELINE

20 March 1980 A moderate earthquake just beneath the volcano is followed by continuing tremors and shocks.
27 March A small crater forms and an ash plume rises.
3 April The authorities declare a State of Emergency.

22 April–7 May Eruptions stop, but a bulge on the north flank of the mountain continues to grow.
7 May Tremors and renewed eruptions of steam and ash.
12 May Small avalanche of rocks caused by earthquake.

18 May, 8.32 am An earthquake causes a huge avalanche on the volcano's north side, immediately followed by an eruption with the force of 55 atomic bombs. The blast is heard 320 km (200 miles) away.

Around ten million trees were flattened like matchsticks, and many were carried into Spirit Lake, covering its surface. It will take up to 200 years for the forests to recover fully.

(1,300°F). This blast overtook the avalanche of debris and swept on, destroying forests and stripping the ground to bare rock in places. Ash as fine as flour fell to earth over 60,000 km² (23,000 sq miles) – it reached New York in three days and circled the world in two weeks. Heat from the eruption melted the ice around the summit, starting massive mudflows. The thick mixture of warmed water and ash slid down the slope like wet concrete, swamping roads and rivers.

Gaping hole

The eruption continued for nine hours, but quickly faded in the evening. By then, the volcano was 400 m (1,300 ft) shorter – its ice-capped peak was gone, leaving a cavern 3 km (2 miles) long and 1.6 km (1 mile) across. There was a series of aftershocks and eruptions throughout 1980, before the mountain eventually calmed down.

Mount St. Helens. The rocky landslide released the enormous pressure inside the volcano, unleashing a massive eruption. Instantly, the bulging side of the mountain shuddered and gave way, hurling out about 3 km³ (¾ cu mile) of rock, snow, and earth at 250 km/h (155 mph). A swirling wind of scorching, shattered lava fragments raced down the mountain, swiftly followed by a scorching cloud that reached temperatures of up to 700°C

> "The entire north side of the summit began sliding north… we were watching this landslide of unbelievable proportions slide down the mountain toward Spirit Lake."
>
> *Geologists Keith and Dorothy Stoffel, in a plane flying over Mount St. Helens at the moment of the blast*

After the eruption, a new cone began to grow in the horseshoe-shaped crater. White plumes of steam regularly poured out in the 1980s.

Volcanologists flocked to Mount St. Helens in 1980 to record the events. Here, they are collecting gas samples.

How devastating?

The Volcanic Explosivity Index (VEI) is a way of comparing the violence of different volcanic eruptions. It is worked out from several factors, including the height of the blast column or plume, the volume of material ejected, and how long the eruption lasts.

VEI 0	Non-explosive eruptions with plume less than 100 m (330 ft); up to 1,000 m³ (35,300 cu ft) of ejecta; variable duration; eg. Kilauea, Hawaii, 1983–
VEI 1	Gentle eruption with plume 100–1,000 m (330–3,300 ft); less than 10,000 m³ (353,000 cu ft) of ejecta; bursts of up to 1 hour; eg. Stromboli, Italy
VEI 2	Explosive eruption with plume 1–5 km (⅔–3 miles); up to 0.01 km³ (0.002 cu miles) of ejecta; lasts 1–6 hours; eg. Colima, Mexico, 1991
VEI 3	Severe eruption with plume 3–15 km (2–9 miles); 0.01–0.1 km³ (0.002–0.02 cu miles) of ejecta; lasts 1–12 hours; eg. Nevado del Ruiz, Colombia, 1985
VEI 4	Cataclysmic eruption with plume 10–25 km (6–15½ miles); 0.1–1 km³ (0.02–0.2 cu miles) of ejecta; lasts 1–12 hours; eg. Sakura-Jima, Japan, 1914
VEI 5	Cataclysmic eruption with plume over 25 km (15½ miles); 1–10 km³ (0.2–2.4 cu miles) of ejecta; lasts 6–12 hours; eg. **Mount St. Helens**, USA, 1980
VEI 6	Colossal eruption with plume over 25 km (15½ miles); 10–100 km³ (2½–24 cu miles) of ejecta; lasts over 12 hours; eg. Krakatau, Indonesia, 1883
VEI 7	Super-colossal eruption with plume over 25 km (15½ miles); 100–1,000 km³ (24–240 cu miles) of ejecta; lasts over 12 hours; eg. Tambora, 1812
VEI 8	Mega-colossal eruption; over 1,000 km³ (240 cu miles) of ejecta; Yellowstone, USA, 640,000 years ago

8:33 am Mount St. Helens blows apart, triggering a pyroclastic blast. Scorching winds of gas and fragmented lava race down the mountainside.
8:30–9.00 am First mudflow starts.

1:30 pm Second mudflow starts.
6:00 pm The eruption finally dies down.
25 May, 12 June, 22 July, 7 August, 16–18 October Further violent eruptions.

1980–1986 A new lava dome grows inside the crater.
September 2004 After violent shuddering, the top of the lava dome starts growing again.
July 2005 The new lava dome collapses.

VOLCANIC ROCK FORMS

Volcanic action, or volcanism, has left many strange rock forms on the landscape. Some are extrusions – made of rock that has been expelled by volcanoes or has seeped out of the ground. Others are intrusions – formed underground by magma that solidified without erupting – and then revealed by erosion or landslides. Some intrusions are massive, stretching over thousands of square kilometres.

Hardened magma from main conduit of an old volcano

Dyke stretches away across desert

Massive, rounded dome of rock

Half of the rock was ground away by glaciers

Half Dome

A batholith is a gigantic lump of granite formed by a vast reservoir of magma hardening under the ground. This one – Half Dome, in the Sierra Nevada mountains – was exposed by uplift and the forces of erosion, which removed the surrounding rock.

Location	Yosemite National Park, California, USA
Age	87 million years
Size	1,440 m (4,735 ft) high
Type	Intrusion

A sill is a horizontal sheet of solid magma

A dyke is a vertical band of solid magma

Sill and dyke, Greece

Dykes follow lines of weakness in the surrounding rock

Dyke swarm, Canada

Alternate layers of different types of solidified magma

Layer dyke, Greenland

Ship Rock

A volcanic neck, such as Ship Rock, can be the only part that remains of an old volcano. It forms when the magma left in a volcano's conduit (central passageway) hardens after an eruption and is left standing when the softer rock of the mountain erodes away. Ridges, called dykes, may spread out from the volcanic neck – these once carried magma from the main conduit into the sides of the volcano. When the volcano was active, the parts we see now were hidden 750–1,000 m (2,500–3,330 ft) below ground.

Location	New Mexico, USA	**Size**	600 m (2,000 ft) high; 500 m (1,670 ft) wide
Age	About 30 million years		
Type	Intrusion		

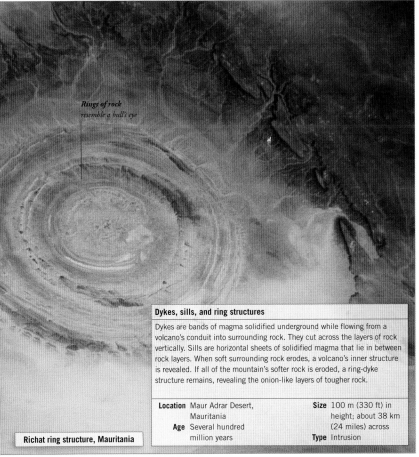

Rings of rock resemble a bull's eye

Dykes, sills, and ring structures

Dykes are bands of magma solidified underground while flowing from a volcano's conduit into surrounding rock. They cut across the layers of rock vertically. Sills are horizontal sheets of solidified magma that lie in between rock layers. When soft surrounding rock erodes, a volcano's inner structure is revealed. If all of the mountain's softer rock is eroded, a ring-dyke structure remains, revealing the onion-like layers of tougher rock.

Location	Maur Adrar Desert, Mauritania	**Size**	100 m (330 ft) in height; about 38 km (24 miles) across
Age	Several hundred million years		
		Type	Intrusion

Richat ring structure, Mauritania

Fairy chimneys

These are small towers of fine-grained volcanic rock called tuff, topped by a chunk of harder rock such as basalt. Tuff erodes easily, but when lumps of hard rock lie on top, they protect the tuff underneath, leaving "chimneys".

Location	Cappadocia, Turkey
Age	Made from tuff created during eruptions 30 million years ago
Size	Up to 50 m (164 ft)
Type	Extrusion

Pillar has been eroded over time

Steep lava sides form a stack

Central vent releases gas, smoke, and further lava

Hornito, at Mount Etna

Lava rising from a flow just beneath the surface may pile up around a vent, creating a mound called a hornito or spatter cone. It forms as lava spurts out under low pressure and falls very close to the vent.

Location	Mount Etna, Sicily, Italy
Age	May form quickly and be short-lived
Size	A few metres
Type	Extrusion

Columns of basalt are hexagonal in shape

Giants' Causeway

Forty thousand stone columns, mostly hexagonal, form the Giant's Causeway. Made of basalt, they are the remains of repeated flows of basalt lava that formed a lava plain. As the lava cooled, it shrank and hardened into columns.

Location	Northern Ireland
Age	Eruption of basalt 60 million years ago
Size	Up to 12 m (40 ft) high and 27 m (90 ft) thick
Type	Extrusion

LIVE VOLCANOES

Some volcanoes sleep for hundreds or even thousands of years. Others are active much more often, and some never stop. There are many active volcanoes around the world. About 20 volcanoes are erupting somewhere on Earth every day, and 60 blast, rumble, or spurt each year. Since records began, about 550 different volcanoes have erupted. An estimated 1,300–1,500 volcanoes have been active during the last 10,000 years.

Lava emerges as fountains and broad rivers

Stromboli

An island volcano off the coast of Sicily, Stromboli has been erupting continuously for at least 2,000 years, and possibly 5,000 years. Small gas explosions hurl lava over the rim several times an hour, but major eruptions are rare. Large Strombolian eruptions with lava flows happen every 2–20 years.

Where	Sicily, Italy
Height	926 m (3,038 ft)
Last eruption	Ongoing
Eruption type	Strombolian
Age	15,000 years

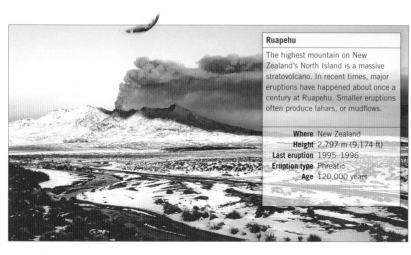

Ruapehu

The highest mountain on New Zealand's North Island is a massive stratovolcano. In recent times, major eruptions have happened about once a century at Ruapehu. Smaller eruptions often produce lahars, or mudflows.

Where	New Zealand
Height	2,797 m (9,174 ft)
Last eruption	1995-1996
Eruption type	Phreatic
Age	120,000 years

Ol Doinyo Lengai

Rising from the African Rift Valley, this is the Earth's only natrocarbonatite volcano. Its unique lava is very runny, like water, and emerges at only 600°C (1,110°F) – so it is cool enough to collect in a metal spoon. It is too cool to glow red, except at night, and is black, hardening to a white powder.

Where	Tanzania
Height	2,890 m (9,482 ft)
Last eruption	2003
Eruption type	Natrocarbonatite
Age	Under 370,000 years

Inactive southern crater is covered in vegetation

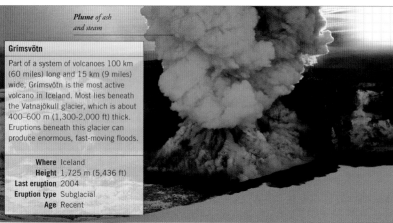

Plume of ash and steam

Grímsvötn

Part of a system of volcanoes 100 km (60 miles) long and 15 km (9 miles) wide, Grímsvötn is the most active volcano in Iceland. Most lies beneath the Vatnajökull glacier, which is about 400–600 m (1,300-2,000 ft) thick. Eruptions beneath this glacier can produce enormous, fast-moving floods.

Where	Iceland
Height	1,725 m (5,436 ft)
Last eruption	2004
Eruption type	Subglacial
Age	Recent

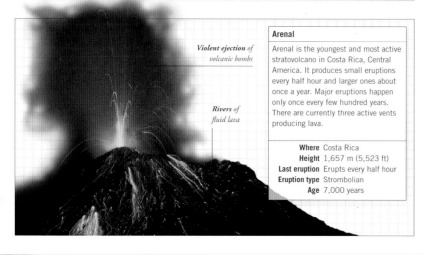

Violent ejection of volcanic bombs

Rivers of fluid lava

Arenal

Arenal is the youngest and most active stratovolcano in Costa Rica, Central America. It produces small eruptions every half hour and larger ones about once a year. Major eruptions happen only once every few hundred years. There are currently three active vents producing lava.

Where	Costa Rica
Height	1,657 m (5,523 ft)
Last eruption	Erupts every half hour
Eruption type	Strombolian
Age	7,000 years

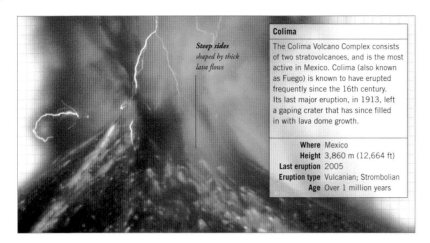

Steep sides
shaped by thick
lava flows

Colima

The Colima Volcano Complex consists of two stratovolcanoes, and is the most active in Mexico. Colima (also known as Fuego) is known to have erupted frequently since the 16th century. Its last major eruption, in 1913, left a gaping crater that has since filled in with lava dome growth.

Where	Mexico
Height	3,860 m (12,664 ft)
Last eruption	2005
Eruption type	Vulcanian; Strombolian
Age	Over 1 million years

Active northern
crater has many
small cones

Hard, old lava
deposits are
white in colour

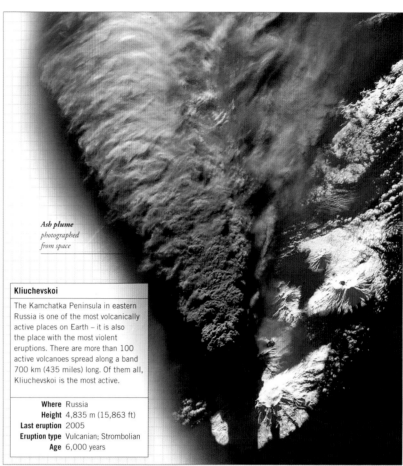

Ash plume
photographed
from space

Kliuchevskoi

The Kamchatka Peninsula in eastern Russia is one of the most volcanically active places on Earth – it is also the place with the most violent eruptions. There are more than 100 active volcanoes spread along a band 700 km (435 miles) long. Of them all, Kliuchevskoi is the most active.

Where	Russia
Height	4,835 m (15,863 ft)
Last eruption	2005
Eruption type	Vulcanian; Strombolian
Age	6,000 years

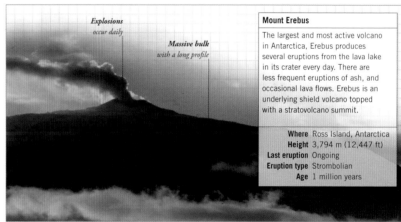

Explosions
occur daily

Massive bulk
with a long profile

Mount Erebus

The largest and most active volcano in Antarctica, Erebus produces several eruptions from the lava lake in its crater every day. There are less frequent eruptions of ash, and occasional lava flows. Erebus is an underlying shield volcano topped with a stratovolcano summit.

Where	Ross Island, Antarctica
Height	3,794 m (12,447 ft)
Last eruption	Ongoing
Eruption type	Strombolian
Age	1 million years

Piton de la Fournaise

Piton de la Fournaise is a vast shield volcano. It shares Réunion Island with another large shield volcano, Piton des Neiges. Both are hotspot volcanoes. Measured from the sea floor where it starts, Piton de la Fournaise rises 6,600 m (21,600 ft).

Where	Réunion Island, Indian Ocean
Height	2,631 m (8,632 ft)
Last eruption	2001
Eruption type	Hawaiian
Age	Over 530,000 years

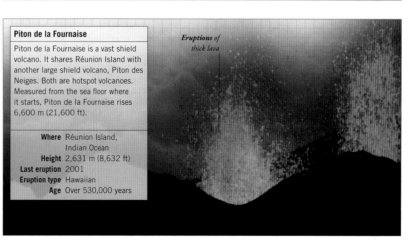

Eruptions of
thick lava

EARTH'S VOLCANOES

Volcanoes are not evenly distributed around the world – most are on the edges of the tectonic plates, with only a few sited in the middle of plates. Most volcanoes are in the sea, where there are many that we do not yet know about.

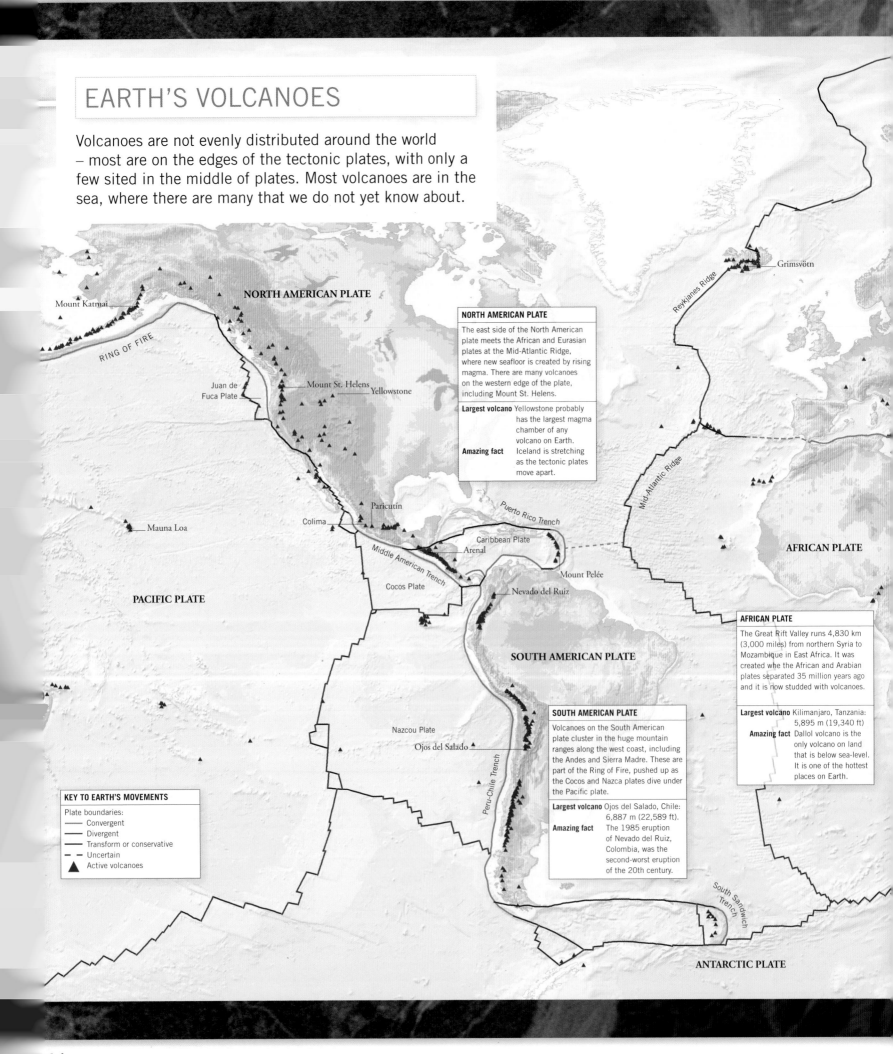

NORTH AMERICAN PLATE

The east side of the North American plate meets the African and Eurasian plates at the Mid-Atlantic Ridge, where new seafloor is created by rising magma. There are many volcanoes on the western edge of the plate, including Mount St. Helens.

Largest volcano Yellowstone probably has the largest magma chamber of any volcano on Earth.

Amazing fact Iceland is stretching as the tectonic plates move apart.

AFRICAN PLATE

The Great Rift Valley runs 4,830 km (3,000 miles) from northern Syria to Mozambique in East Africa. It was created whe the African and Arabian plates separated 35 million years ago and it is now studded with volcanoes.

Largest volcano Kilimanjaro, Tanzania: 5,895 m (19,340 ft)

Amazing fact Dallol volcano is the only volcano on land that is below sea-level. It is one of the hottest places on Earth.

SOUTH AMERICAN PLATE

Volcanoes on the South American plate cluster in the huge mountain ranges along the west coast, including the Andes and Sierra Madre. These are part of the Ring of Fire, pushed up as the Cocos and Nazca plates dive under the Pacific plate.

Largest volcano Ojos del Salado, Chile: 6,887 m (22,589 ft).

Amazing fact The 1985 eruption of Nevado del Ruiz, Colombia, was the second-worst eruption of the 20th century.

KEY TO EARTH'S MOVEMENTS

Plate boundaries:
— Convergent
— Divergent
— Transform or conservative
-- Uncertain
▲ Active volcanoes

Mount Katmai
NORTH AMERICAN PLATE
RING OF FIRE
Juan de Fuca Plate
Mount St. Helens
Yellowstone
Mauna Loa
Paricutín
Colima
Middle American Trench
Cocos Plate
PACIFIC PLATE
Puerto Rico Trench
Caribbean Plate
Arenal
Mount Pelée
Nevado del Ruiz
SOUTH AMERICAN PLATE
Nazcou Plate
Ojos del Salado
Peru-Chile Trench
ANTARCTIC PLATE
South Sandwich Trench
AFRICAN PLATE
Mid-Atlantic Ridge
Reykjanes Ridge
Grimsvötn

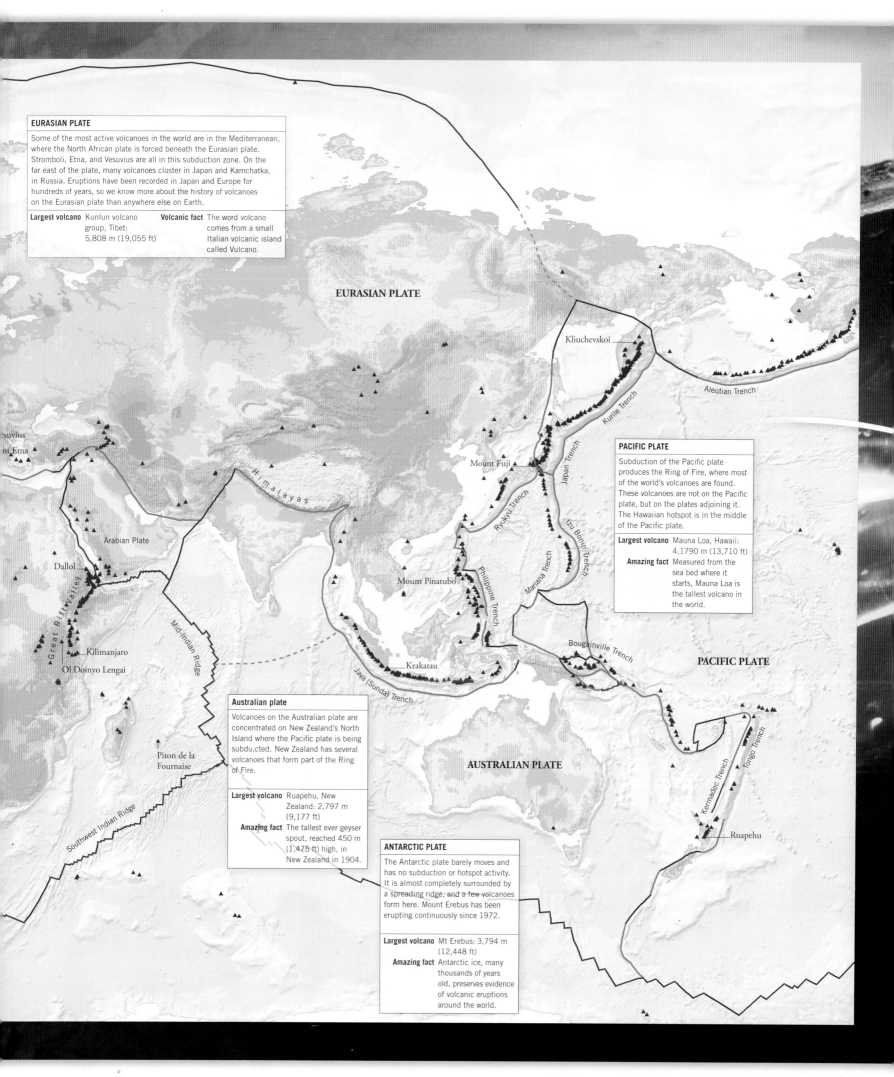

EURASIAN PLATE

Some of the most active volcanoes in the world are in the Mediterranean, where the North African plate is forced beneath the Eurasian plate. Stromboli, Etna, and Vesuvius are all in this subduction zone. On the far east of the plate, many volcanoes cluster in Japan and Kamchatka, in Russia. Eruptions have been recorded in Japan and Europe for hundreds of years, so we know more about the history of volcanoes on the Eurasian plate than anywhere else on Earth.

Largest volcano Kunlun volcano group, Tibet: 5,808 m (19,055 ft)

Volcanic fact The word volcano comes from a small Italian volcanic island called Vulcano.

EURASIAN PLATE

Kliuchevskoi

Aleutian Trench

Kurile Trench

Vesuvius

Mt Etna

Arabian Plate

Dallol

Japan Trench

Mount Fuji

PACIFIC PLATE

Subduction of the Pacific plate produces the Ring of Fire, where most of the world's volcanoes are found. These volcanoes are not on the Pacific plate, but on the plates adjoining it. The Hawaiian hotspot is in the middle of the Pacific plate.

Largest volcano Mauna Loa, Hawaii: 4,1790 m (13,710 ft)

Amazing fact Measured from the sea bed where it starts, Mauna Loa is the tallest volcano in the world.

Himalayas

Ryukyu Trench

Izu Bonin Trench

Mariana Trench

Great Rift Valley

Kilimanjaro

Ol Doinyo Lengai

Mid-Indian Ridge

Mount Pinatubo

Philippine Trench

Bougainville Trench

PACIFIC PLATE

Krakatau

Java (Sunda) Trench

Piton de la Fournaise

Australian plate

Volcanoes on the Australian plate are concentrated on New Zealand's North Island where the Pacific plate is being subdu,cted. New Zealand has several volcanoes that form part of the Ring of Fire.

Largest volcano Ruapehu, New Zealand: 2,797 m (9,177 ft)

Amazing fact The tallest ever geyser spout, reached 450 m (1,475 ft) high, in New Zealand in 1904.

Southwest Indian Ridge

AUSTRALIAN PLATE

Kermadec Trench

Tongo Trench

Ruapehu

ANTARCTIC PLATE

The Antarctic plate barely moves and has no subduction or hotspot activity. It is almost completely surrounded by a spreading ridge, and a few volcanoes form here. Mount Erebus has been erupting continuously since 1972.

Largest volcano Mt Erebus: 3,794 m (12,448 ft)

Amazing fact Antarctic ice, many thousands of years old, preserves evidence of volcanic eruptions around the world.

65

INDEX

ACKNOWLEDGEMENTS

For Cliff Knight, with thanks

Dorling Kindersley would like to thank Polly Boyd for proof-reading; Hilary Bird for the index; Christine Heilman for text Americanization; Dr. Andrew Coburn, Vice President of Catastrophe Research, Risk Management Solutions Inc, and Ron Rooney, Fellow of the Royal Institue of Chemistry, for additional help and advice.

Picture Credits
The publishers would like to thank the following for their kind permission to reproduce their photographs:

(Abbreviations key: r= right; l= left; a= above; b= below; c= centre; bckgrd= background.)

2 Getty Images: Richard A. Cooke c. **4 Getty Images:** Richard A. Cooke c. **6 Corbis:** North Carolina Museum of Art t; Sean Sexton Collection cr. **6 Getty Images:** Richard A. Cooke bckgrd. **7 Corbis:** Bettmann bl, br; Jonathan Blair t. **11 Illustrator's reference: www.historyoftheuniverse.com:** tr. **12 © The Natural History Museum, London:** bla. **15 Zefa Visual Media UK Ltd:** J.F. Raga br. **19 Science Photo Library:** Dr Ken Macdonald br. **21 Corbis:** Dave Bartruff b. **24 Corbis:** cr. **24 Mary Evans Picture Library:** bl. **25 Circus World Museum:** Image courtesy of Circus World Museum, Wisconsin/permission from Ringling Bros. & Barnum and Bailey bl. **25 Corbis:** cl; Philip Gould tr. **28 Getty Images:** AFP tc; G. Brad Lewis tr. **29 Corbis:** Paul A. Souders tc. **29 Science Photo Library:** G. Brad Lewis tl. **31 © Michael Holford:** tr. **35 Empics Ltd:** PA Photos tr. **36 Corbis:** David Muench b. **37 Frans Lanting Photography:** www.lanting. com c. **38 DK Images:** Instituto Nacional de Antropologia e Historia/Michel Zabe bcl. **38 Glendale Community College, Arizona, U.S.A:** Courtesy of Stan Celestian tr, cl, c, cb. **38 Frans Lanting Photography:** www.lanting.com bckgrd. **39 Corbis:** tr, Vittoriano Rastelli br. **39 Empics Ltd:** PA Photos cr. **40 Corbis:** Gunter Marx Photography tr. **41 National Geographic Image Collection:** Raymond Gehman bl. **41 NASA:** Courtesy of Image Analysis Lab, NASA Johnson Space Center/http://eol.jsc.nasa.gov/STS040-614-63 tr. **47 Courtesy of www.digitalglobe.com:** tr. **48 Corbis:** Bettmann c. **48 OSF/photolibrary.com:** Mary Plage tl. **49 Alamy Images:** Eric Chahi br. **49 Images de Volcans/ Maurice and Katia Krafft:** tl. **50 Corbis:** Yann Arthus-Bertrand cr; Jonathan Blair cl. **50 NASA:** Landsat image courtesy of Smithsonian Institute tr. **50 National Geographic Image Collection:** Wilbur Garrett bl. **51 Corbis:** Jonathan Blair cr; Danny Lehman tl; NASA/Roger Ressmeyer br. **51 OSF/photolibrary.com:** Carini Joe tr. **55 Science Photo Library:** David Scharf t. **56 Getty Images:** Astromujoff c.

57 Rex Features: tr. **57 Science Photo Library:** NOAA/ Robert M. Carey cr. **58 Getty Images:** Astromujoff bckgrd. **58 U.S. Geological Survey:** br; Gary Rosenquist l. **59 U.S. Geological Survey:** tl, tr. **60 Corbis:** br; Peter Guttman bc; Danny Lehman tr. **60 Geological Survey of Canada:** Dr Robert H. Rainbird cb. **60 Getty Images:** Astromujoff bckgrd. **60 National Geographic Image Collection:** Randy Olson l. **60 Tom Pfeiffer:** www.decadevolcano.net c. **61 Corbis:** Ric Ergenbright br. **61 Getty Images:** Robert Frerck tr. **61 Images de Volcans/Maurice and Katia Krafft:** cr. **62 Corbis:** Sygma/ Alfio Scigliano tr. **62 Getty Images:** Astromujoff bckgrd. **62 N.H.P.A.:** Kevin Schafer bl. **62 Rex Features:** tl. **62 Mats Wibe Lund:** cl. **63 Corbis:** Sygma/JIR br. **63 OSF/photolibrary.com:** Doug Allan cr; NASA tr. **63 Reuters:** Eduardo Quiros tl. **63 Science Photo Library:** Bernhard Edmaier bl. **64 Getty Images:** Astromujoff bckgrd. **65 Getty Images:** Richard A. Cooke bckgrd. **66 Getty Images:** Richard A. Cooke c. **68 Getty Images:** Richard A. Cooke c. **70 Getty Images:** Richard A. Cooke c.

Text Credits
The publishers would like to thank the following for their kind permission to reproduce their extracts:

6, l Penguin Books Ltd: from *The Letters of The Younger Pliny* p167, translated with an introduction by Betty Radice (Penguin Classics 1963, Reprinted 1969). Copyright © Betty Radice, 1963, 1969. Reproduced by permission of Penguin Books Ltd. **24, 25, 58, 59 Yale University Press:** from *Vulcan's Fury* pp164, 172, 216, 218, by Alwyn Scarth (Yale University Press, 1999). Copyright © 1999 by Alwyn Scarth.

Every effort has been made to trace all copyright holders. The publishers will be pleased to hear from any copyright holders not here acknowledged.

LONDON, NEW YORK, MELBOURNE,
MUNICH, AND DELHI

Consultant Douglas Palmer

Senior Editor Jayne Miller
Senior Art Editor Smiljka Surla
Editors Sarah Larter, Jackie Fortey, Ben Hoare
Designers Johnny Pau, Rebecca Wright

Managing Editor Camilla Hallinan
Managing Art Editor Sophia M. Tampakopoulos Turner

DTP Coordinator Siu Yin Chan, Natasha Lu

Publishing Managers Caroline Buckingham, Andrew Macintyre
Category Publisher Laura Buller, Jonathan Metcalf

Picture Research Bridget Tily
Production Erica Rosen
Jacket Design Neal Cobourne

Illustrators Atlantic Digital, Candy Lab, Andrew Kerr

First published in Great Britian in 2006 by
Dorling Kindersley Limited,
80 Strand, London WC2R 0RL

A CIP catalogue record for this book
is available from the British Library

ISBN 1 4053 0861 3

Colour reproduction by Colourscan, Singapore
Printed and bound in China by Hung Hing

Discover more at
www.dk.com